Revenue Statistics in Asian Countries

TRENDS IN INDONESIA, JAPAN, KAZAKHSTAN, KOREA, MALAYSIA, THE PHILIPPINES AND SINGAPORE

This work is published under the responsibility of the Secretary-General of the OECD. The opinions expressed and arguments employed herein do not necessarily reflect the official views of the member countries of the OECD or its Development Centre.

This document, as well as any data and map included herein, are without prejudice to the status of or sovereignty over any territory, to the delimitation of international frontiers and boundaries and to the name of any territory, city or area.

Please cite this publication as:

OECD (2017), *Revenue Statistics in Asian Countries: Trends in Indonesia, Japan, Kazakhstan, Korea, Malaysia, the Philippines and Singapore*, OECD Publishing, Paris.
http://dx.doi.org/10.1787/9789264278943-en

ISBN 978-92-64-27893-6 (print)
ISBN 978-92-64-27894-3 (PDF)
ISBN 978-92-64-27902-5 (ePub)

Corrigenda to OECD publications may be found on line at: *www.oecd.org/publishing/corrigenda.htm*

Foreword

Revenue Statistics in Asian Countries: Trends in Indonesia, Japan, Kazakhstan, Korea, Malaysia, the Philippines and Singapore *is a joint publication by the OECD Centre for Tax Policy and Administration and the OECD Development Centre. It presents detailed, internationally comparable data on tax revenues for seven Asian economies, two of which (Korea and Japan) are OECD members. Its approach is based on the well-established methodology of the OECD Revenue Statistics, which has become an essential reference source for OECD member countries. Comparisons are also made with the average for OECD economies and Latin American and Caribbean (LAC) countries.*

In this publication, the term "taxes" is confined to compulsory, unrequited payments to general government. As outlined in the Interpretative Guide to the Revenue Statistics, taxes are "unrequited" in the sense that benefits provided by government to taxpayers are not normally in proportion to their payments. The OECD methodology classifies a tax according to its base: income, profits and capital gains (classified under heading 1000), payroll (heading 3000), property (heading 4000), goods and services (heading 5000) and other taxes (heading 6000). Compulsory social security contributions paid to general government are treated as taxes, and are classified under heading 2000. Much greater detail on the tax concept, the classification of taxes and the accrual basis of reporting is set out in the Interpretative Guide in Annex A.

Extending the OECD methodology to Asian countries makes possible comparisons of tax systems on a consistent basis between countries in Asia, Africa, Latin America and the Caribbean and the OECD.

The report also provides an overview of the main taxation trends in Indonesia, Japan, Kazakhstan, Korea, Malaysia, the Philippines and Singapore. It examines changes in both the levels and the composition of tax revenues plus the attribution by sub-level of government between 1990 and 2015.

The report also includes a special feature which discusses the development and use of electronic services in tax administrations in Asia.

Acknowledgements

Revenue Statistics in Asian Countries: Trends in Indonesia, Japan, Kazakhstan, Korea, Malaysia, the Philippines and Singapore is jointly produced by the Organisation for Economic Co-operation and Development (OECD) Centre for Tax Policy and Administration and the OECD Development Centre. The staff from these two entities with responsibility for producing the publication were: Kensuke Tanaka, Head of Asia Desk, Jingjing Xia, Statistician/Policy Analyst and Prasiwi Ibrahim, Economist at the OECD Development Centre under the supervision of the Director Mario Pezzini; Michelle Harding, Head, Tax Data and Statistical Analysis, Emmanuelle Modica, Statistician/Analyst, and Osamu Yoshida, Deputy Head, Global Relations of the OECD Centre for Tax Policy and Administration under the supervision of the Director Pascal Saint-Amans, Deputy Director Grace Perez-Navarro and the Head of the Tax Policy and Tax Statistics Division David Bradbury. The special feature benefited from useful inputs from the Asian Development Bank (ADB), provided by Donghyun Park, Principal Economist and Yuji Miyaki, Public Management Specialist.

The authors would like to thank other staff at the OECD Development Centre and the Centre for Tax Policy and Administration for their invaluable help in completing this publication. Elizabeth Nash and Delphine Grandrieux from the OECD Development Centre's Communications and Publications team ensured the production of the publication, in both paper and electronic form. Support was also provided by Rintaro Tamaki, Deputy Secretary-General of the OECD as well as Koichoro Aritoshi, Rokiah Bakar, Assel Baltabayeva, Dariya Bissengaliyeva, Gil Beltran, Rowena Sta Clara, Meirbekov Daniyar, Kenneth Lee, Zhi Wei Lim, Datuk Haji Mohd Esa Abd Manaf, Brian McAuley, Teresa Mendoza, Amir Abdul Mutalib Shaari, Rena Nagayama, Hui Li Ng, Kunta Nugraha, Kumara Candra Ratri Raden, Jiehui Shen, Adzhar Sulaiman, Joanne Tan, Mui Choo Teng, Suryani Widarta, Zarina Yerkebayeva, Dauren Zakumbayev, Marsidi Zelika. The Centre for Tax Policy and Administration and the Development Centre gratefully acknowledge financial support from the government of Japan. Finally, the authors are also very grateful to colleagues working in national governments with whom they consulted regularly. These institutions include the finance ministries of Indonesia, Japan, Kazakhstan, Korea, the Philippines, Singapore and the Inland Revenue Board of Malaysia.

* This document was produced with the financial assistance of the European Union. The views expressed herein can in no way be taken to reflect the official opinion of the European Union.

Table of contents

Executive summary   9

Chapter 1. Tax revenue trends, 1990-2015   13

   1.1. Tax ratios.   14
   1.2. Tax structures.   25
   1.3. Taxes by level of government.   32
   1.4. Comparative figures   34
   Notes.   35
   References   35

Chapter 2. SPECIAL FEATURE: Electronic services in tax administration   39

   2.1. Successfully harnessing ICT opportunities presents numerous challenges
      for revenue bodies   40
   2.2. Use of electronic filing for key tax types   41
   2.3. Using electronic payment methods for collecting taxes   43
   2.4. Progress of electronic tax services in Southeast Asian countries
      and Kazakhstan   45
   References   47

Chapter 3. Tax levels and tax structures, 1990-2015   49

   3.1. Comparative tables, 1990-2015.   50
   3.2. Comparative figures   57

Chapter 4. Country tables, 1997-2015 – Tax revenues   59

Annex A. The OECD Interpretative Guide   77

Tables

   1.1. Attribution of tax revenues to sub-sectors of general government
      as % of total tax revenue, 2015.   32
   2.1. Strategic priorities for increased use of online services   41
   2.2. Rates of electronic tax filing for the major taxes, 2011 and 2013   43
   2.3. Tax payment methods available and volume usage, 2013.   44
   3.1. Total tax revenue as percentage of GDP, 1990-2015   51
   3.2. Tax revenue of main headings as percentage of GDP, 2015   51
   3.3. Tax revenue of main headings as percentage of total taxation, 2015   52
   3.4. Taxes on income and profits (1000) as percentage of GDP.   52
   3.5. Taxes on income and profits (1000) as percentage of total taxation   52
   3.6. Social security contributions (2000) as percentage of GDP   53

3.7. Social security contributions (2000) as percentage of total taxation 53
3.8. Taxes on property (4000) as percentage of GDP. 53
3.9. Taxes on property (4000) as percentage of total taxation 54
3.10. Taxes on goods and services (5000) as percentage of GDP. 54
3.11. Taxes on goods and services (5000) as percentage of total taxation 54
3.12. Taxes on general consumption (5110) as percentage of GDP 54
3.13. Taxes on general consumption (5110) as percentage of total taxation 55
3.14. Taxes on specific goods and services (5120) as percentage of GDP 55
3.15. Taxes on specific goods and services (5120) as percentage of total taxation . . . 55
3.16. Gross domestic product for tax reporting years at market prices,
       in billions of national currency units 56
3.17. Gross domestic product for tax reporting years at market prices,
       in millions of US Dollars at market exchange rates 56
3.18. Total tax revenue in millions of US dollars at market exchange rates 56
3.19. Exchange rates used, national currency per US dollar. 56
4.1. Indonesia 60
4.2. Japan 62
4.3. Kazakhstan. 65
4.4. Korea 67
4.5. Malaysia 71
4.6. Philippines 73
4.7. Singapore 75

Figures

1.1. Tax-to-GDP ratios (total tax revenue as % of GDP), 2015 15
1.2. Tax-to-GDP ratios and GDP per capita (in PPP) in Asian countries, Latin America
     and the Caribbean, OECD and African countries, 2015. 16
1.3. Annual changes in tax-to-GDP ratios (p.p.), 2015 17
1.4. Net changes in tax-to-GDP ratios between 2014 and 2015 by main type
     of taxes (p.p.) 17
1.5. Tax-to-GDP ratios (%), 1990-2015. 18
1.6. Agriculture as % of GDP and tax-to-GDP ratios, 2015 20
1.7. Changes in tax-to-GDP ratios by type of taxes between 2000 and 2015 (p.p.). . . 21
1.8. Net changes in tax-to-GDP ratios between 2000 and 2015 by main type
     of taxes (p.p.) 22
1.9. Tax revenue by main type of taxes as % of GDP, 2015. 23
1.10. Corporate income tax revenue as % of GDP in Indonesia, 2000-15. 24
1.11. Corporate income tax rates in Indonesia, 2000-15 24
1.12. Corporate income tax revenue as % of GDP in Kazakhstan, 2000-15 24
1.13. Corporate income tax rates in Kazakhstan, 2000-15 24
1.14. Corporate income tax revenue as % of GDP in Singapore, 2000-15. 25
1.15. Corporate income tax rates in Singapore, 2000-15 25
1.16. Tax structures (as % of total tax revenue), 2015 26
1.17. Revenue from taxes on general consumption as % of total tax revenue,
      2000 and 2015. 26
1.18. Revenue from taxes on specific goods and services as % of total tax revenue,
      2000 and 2015 26

1.19. Revenue from excises as % of total tax revenue, 2000 and 2015 27

1.20. Revenue from customs and import duties as % of total tax revenue,
2000 and 2015 27

1.21. Revenue from VAT as % of total tax revenue, 2000 and 2015 28

1.22. Revenue from corporate income tax and personal income tax as % of total tax
revenue, 2015 29

1.23. VAT revenue ratio (VRR) in Asian countries (%), 2014 30

1.24. VAT revenue ratio (VRR) in Asian countries (%), 1990-2014 31

1.25. Composition of local government tax revenue by main type of taxes, 2015 33

1.26. Tax structures, 2015 34

3.1. Tax revenue of main headings as % of total tax revenue, 2015 57

3.2. Tax structures, 1990-2015 58

Follow OECD Publications on:

 *http://twitter.com/OECD_Pubs*

 *http://www.facebook.com/OECDPublications*

 *http://www.linkedin.com/groups/OECD-Publications-4645871*

 *http://www.youtube.com/oecdilibrary*

 *http://www.oecd.org/oecddirect/*

This book has...

 *StatLinks*
A service that delivers Excel® files from the printed page!

Look for the *StatLinks* at the bottom of the tables or graphs in this book. To download the matching Excel® spreadsheet, just type the link into your Internet browser, starting with the *http://dx.doi.org* prefix, or click on the link from the e-book edition.

Executive summary

Revenue Statistics in Asian Countries provides internationally comparable data on tax levels and tax structures for seven Asian countries: Indonesia, Japan, Kazakhstan, Korea, Malaysia, the Philippines and Singapore. It also includes a special feature, which discusses the development of information and communications technology (ICT) in tax administrations in Asia.

Tax-to-GDP ratios in Asian countries range from 11.8% in Indonesia to over 32.0% in Japan, with all countries other than Japan and Korea below 18% (data for Japan is for 2014 due to data unavailability). Ratios in all countries are lower than the OECD average of 34.3% in 2015. Tax-to-GDP ratios are defined as total tax revenue, including social security contributions (SSCs), as a percentage of gross domestic product (GDP).

In this publication, "taxes" are defined as compulsory, unrequited payments to general government. Taxes are "unrequited" in the sense that benefits provided by government to taxpayers are not normally in proportion to their payments. The OECD methodology classifies a tax according to its base: income, profits and capital gains, payroll, property, goods and services and other taxes. Compulsory SSCs paid to general government are classified as taxes. More information on the tax classification and the basis of reporting is set out in the Interpretative Guide in Annex A.

Changes in tax-to-GDP ratios in Asian countries in 2015

Facing a range of external and domestic challenges, the growth of Asian economies was moderate in 2015. Major external shocks affecting economic activity in the region included the significant drop in global commodity prices, China's economic slowdown, and the slower recovery in advanced countries. Between 2014 and 2015, the tax-to-GDP ratio continued to decrease in Indonesia, Kazakhstan and Malaysia. The ratio also decreased in Singapore, although it still remained higher than its 2013 level. The decrease between 2014 and 2015 was particularly significant in Kazakhstan (5.6 percentage points, compared to less than 0.7 percentage points in the other countries), due mainly to a fall in oil tax revenues. Korea saw the largest increase over this period of 0.7 percentage points.

Since 2000, the tax-to-GDP ratio has increased in five of the Asian countries featured in this publication, primarily due to tax reforms and the modernisation of tax systems and administrations. The increases between 2000 and 2015 ranged from 0.7 percentage points in Malaysia to 3.8 percentage points in Korea. Kazakhstan and Singapore decreased their tax-to-GDP ratios by 4.3 percentage points and 1.9 percentage points respectively over this period. Falling corporate tax revenues as a percentage of GDP, partially due to changes in corporate income tax rates, contributed to this decrease.

The main drivers of the growth in tax-to-GDP ratios since 2000 differed across the countries concerned. Revenue from taxes on income and profits was the predominant driver of growth in Malaysia and the Philippines, whereas in Indonesia the growth in its tax-to-GDP ratio was principally driven by the growth in revenues from taxes on goods and services. In Korea and Japan, the biggest increase since 2000 occurred in SSCs, which accounted for over 3 percentage points in both countries.

Tax structures in Asian countries in 2015

Excluding Japan and Korea, the countries in this publication rely more heavily on corporate taxes and less heavily on SSCs and value added tax (VAT) than the Latin American and Caribbean (LAC) and OECD averages, with the partial exception of Indonesia, where VAT revenue is higher. In contrast, the tax structures of Japan and Korea are more evenly split between the main categories of tax revenues in 2015, similar to the OECD average.

- In 2015, revenue from taxes on income and profits in Malaysia reached 59.6% of total taxation whereas this category amounted to between 40% and 45% in the other Southeast Asian countries, 38.8% in Kazakhstan and between 30% and 35% in Korea, Japan (in 2014) and the OECD countries on average (in 2014).

- In 2015, corporate income taxes were a significant source of tax revenue in all seven countries, ranging from 12.8% of total taxation in Korea to 42.5% in Malaysia, compared to the OECD average of 8.8%. As a percentage of GDP, corporate income tax revenues in Japan, Korea, Malaysia and the Philippines were higher in 2015 than in 2000, despite reductions in corporate income tax rates over this period.

- The share of VAT as a proportion of total tax revenues in 2015 remained smaller (except for Indonesia) than the OECD average of 20.1% (in 2014) due to generally lower VAT rates, ranging from 12.2% in Japan (in 2014) to 18.6% in Singapore. In Indonesia the share of VAT as a percentage of total tax revenues amounted to 31.1% in 2015.

- Revenues from SSCs are relatively small in Southeast Asian countries and Kazakhstan, ranging from 1.6% of total taxation in Malaysia to 14.0% in the Philippines. The figures for SSCs in Indonesia are not available, but are negligible. Singapore does not levy any SSCs. In contrast, SSCs represent more than 25% on average in the OECD (including Japan and Korea).

VAT revenue ratios in 2014

VAT revenue ratios (VRRs) in Asian countries varied in 2014. A VRR of 100% would suggest that all VAT is collected on its entire potential base and there is no loss of VAT revenue as a consequence of exemptions, reduced rates, fraud, evasion or tax planning. The Philippines and Kazakhstan had the lowest VRRs, at below 50% in both cases, whereas Singapore had the highest at 84%. Japan, Korea and Singapore had relatively high VRRs, exceeding 65%. The VRR has not changed significantly for Japan, Korea and Singapore since 2000, whereas it has experienced major changes in Indonesia and Kazakhstan over that period, increasing by 23 percentage points in Indonesia and by 14 percentage points in Kazakhstan.

Special feature: Information and communications technology (ICT) in tax administrations in Asia

The level of tax revenues in an economy is influenced by tax policy and administration as well as taxpayer compliance and government enforcement. Recent developments in information and communications technology (ICT), both for electronic filing and for payment of taxes, have presented many opportunities for revenue bodies to increase government revenue, improve efficiency, and enhance the quality of services delivered to taxpayers. At the same time they have enabled an overall reduction in taxpayer compliance costs and government administration costs, while delivering improved enforcement.

Chapter 1

Tax revenue trends, 1990-2015

1.1. Tax ratios

In light of the United Nation's 2030 Agenda for Sustainable Development, awareness of the need to mobilise government revenue in developing countries to fund public goods and services is increasing. Taxation provides a predictable and sustainable source of government revenue, in contrast with declining development assistance and the volatility of non-tax revenues with respect to commodity prices.

This report presents detailed internationally comparable data on tax revenues of seven Asian countries: Indonesia, Japan, Kazakhstan, Korea, Malaysia, the Philippines and Singapore. This chapter discusses the key tax indicators for this group of countries: the tax-to-GDP ratio, the tax structure and the share of tax revenue by level of government. The discussion supplements the detailed country information found in Chapter 4.

Tax-to-GDP ratios in 2015

The tax-to-GDP ratio is the total tax revenue of a country (including social security contributions) measured as a proportion of the gross domestic product (GDP). In 2015, tax-to-GDP ratios in the seven countries included in this publication ranged from 11.8% in Indonesia to 25.3% in Korea. In Japan, the tax-to-GDP ratio in 2014 was 32.0%, the highest of the countries included in this publication.[1] Korea and Japan have relatively high tax-to-GDP ratio (above 25%) compared to Indonesia, Kazakhstan, Malaysia, the Philippines and Singapore (below 18%), as shown in Figure 1.1. The higher tax-to-GDP ratios in Korea and Japan are partially due to their more diversified economies, which make them more able to collect tax revenue from various economic sectors (Papageorgiou et al, 2015).

The tax-to-GDP ratios in Indonesia, Kazakhstan, Malaysia, the Philippines and Singapore in 2015 were 11.8%, 15.5%, 15.3%, 17.0% and 13.6% of GDP respectively. In the Philippines and Indonesia, the governments are endeavouring to strengthen their tax revenues and have established tax-to-GDP targets. The Philippines aims to increase their tax-to-GDP ratio to 17% (excluding social security contributions) by 2016 (The Philippine Star, 2016) and Indonesia aims to reach the same level by 2019 (OECD, 2015a). These targets will contribute to increasing financial capacity toward the minimum tax-to-GDP ratio of 25% deemed essential to become a developed country (UNESCAP, 2014).

Tax-to-GDP ratios tend to be higher in high-income countries: in general, OECD countries collect a higher amount of tax revenues than non-OECD countries, measured as a percentage of GDP. Asian and Latin American and Caribbean countries have broadly similar income and development levels and similar tax-to-GDP ratios. This is illustrated in Figure 1.2, which shows the tax-to-GDP ratios and GDP per capita of the seven countries of this publication compared with Latin American and Caribbean, African and OECD countries.

Singapore has the highest GDP per-capita of the seven countries and one of the lowest tax-to-GDP ratios. The high GDP per capita in Singapore results from significant inward flows of foreign direct investment (FDI) due to a highly attractive business climate and a stable political environment (UNCTAD, 2012). The low tax-to-GDP ratio is explained by lower income tax rates (particularly on corporate income) and VAT rates, compared to other Asian countries (UNESCAP, 2014).

Figure 1.1. **Tax-to-GDP ratios (total tax revenue as % of GDP), 2015**

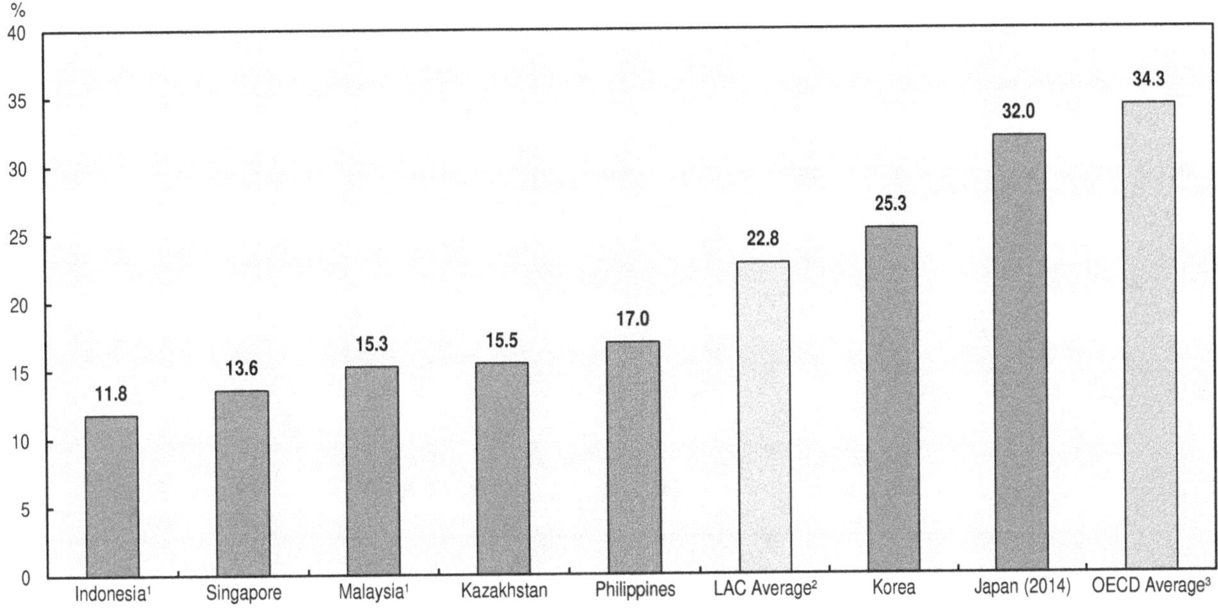

Note: Data for Korea, Japan and the OECD average are taken from Revenue Statistics (OECD, 2016a) and are preliminary for 2015, except for Japan, where some 2015 data are not available.
1. The figures exclude state government revenues for Malaysia and social security contributions for Indonesia.
2. Represents the unweighted average for 24 LAC (Latin American and Caribbean) countries.
3. Represents the unweighted average for OECD member countries. Japan and Korea are also part of the OECD (35) group.
Source: Table 3.1.

StatLink http://dx.doi.org/10.1787/888933543296

In the Southeast Asia region, tax-to-GDP ratios tend to be lower compared to Japan and Korea. This is explained by two main factors: low tax compliance in many countries (UNESCAP, 2016) with the notable exception of Singapore, where tax compliance is high; and narrow tax bases due to numerous tax exemptions and incentives to attract foreign investment (UNESCAP, 2014). In Indonesia, for example, an estimated 44 million people should be paying tax whereas only 27 million are registered and less than 40% of them pay the full amount of income tax (UNESCAP, 2016).

Evolution of tax-to-GDP ratios

The evolution of tax-to-GDP ratios has been different in each country between 2014 and 2015 (Figure 1.3). Kazakhstan and the Southeast Asian countries with the exception of the Philippines saw decreases in their tax-to-GDP ratios. Kazakhstan experienced the largest decrease of 5.6 percentage points (p.p.) from 2014 to 2015, largely explained by the drop in oil tax revenues which decreased by 4.5 p.p. following the collapse of global oil prices. Changes in the Southeast Asian countries are relatively small from an increase of 0.3 p.p. in the Philippines to a decrease of 0.6 p.p. in Malaysia. Among the six countries included in this publication (except Japan which has no tax-to-GDP data in 2015), Korea has seen the largest increase, at 0.7 p.p.

Figure 1.2. **Tax-to-GDP ratios and GDP per capita (in PPP) in Asian countries, Latin America and the Caribbean, OECD and African countries, 2015**

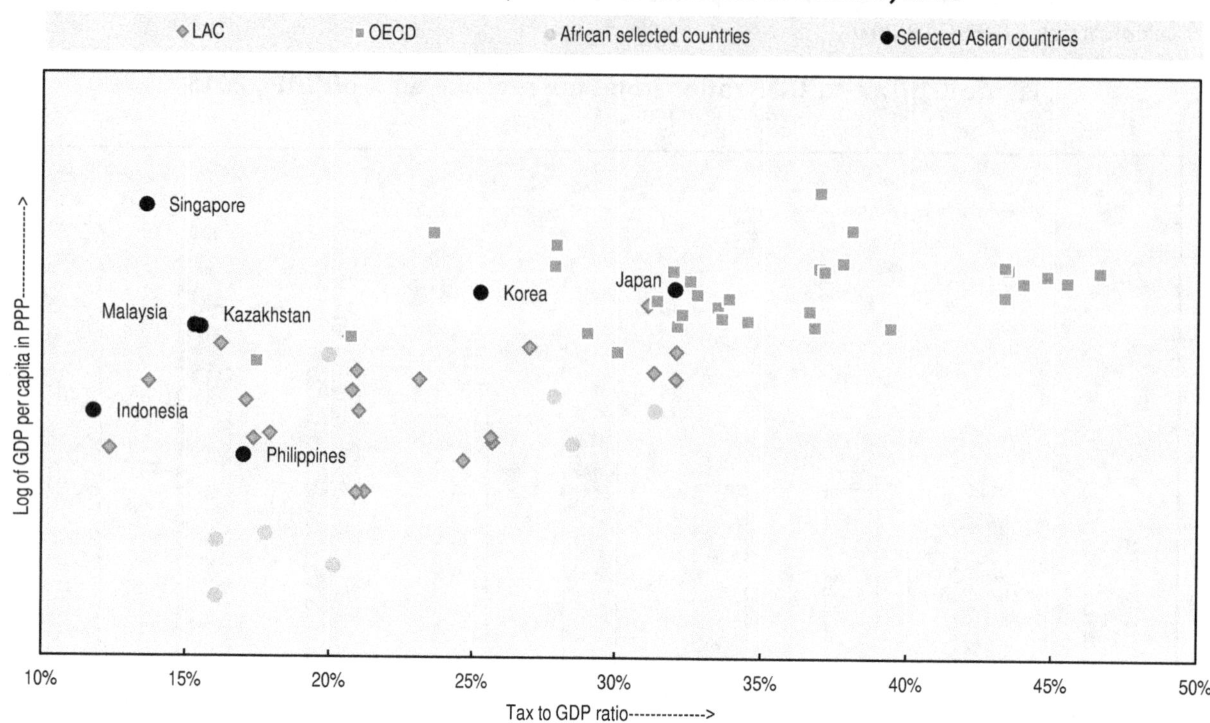

Note: The y-axis is on a logarithmic scale. Tax-to-GDP ratios for Japan and the selected African countries refer to 2014 as data in 2015 are not available. The purchasing-power-parity (PPP) between two countries is the rate at which the currency of one country needs to be converted into that of a second country to ensure that a given amount of the first country's currency will purchase the same volume of goods and services in the second country as it does in the first. The implied PPP conversion rate is expressed as national currency per current international dollar. An international dollar has the same purchasing power as the US dollar has in the United States. An international dollar is a hypothetical currency that is used as a means of translating and comparing costs from one country to the other using a common reference point, the US dollar (Definitions derived from IMF, 2016 and WHO, 2015).

Source: IMF (2016), *World Economic Outlook*, October 2016, International Monetary Fund for figures of GDP per capita. Tax-to-GDP ratios are sourced from the regional Revenue Statistics publications (*www.oecd.org/tax/taxpolicy/revenue-statistics-comparable-tax-revenue-data.htm*).

StatLink 𝍌𝍈𝍖 *http://dx.doi.org/10.1787/888933543315*

By further distinguishing the changes in tax-to-GDP ratio by main type of taxes, the biggest contributors to the changes are revenues from taxes on income, profits and capital gains as well as taxes on specific goods and services. These revenues decreased in Kazakhstan by 1.8 p.p. and 3.1 p.p. respectively. In Malaysia, the 1.8 p.p. increase in revenues from general taxes on goods and services was offset by declines in revenues from taxes on income, profits and capital gains. Indonesia and Singapore have similar changes with increases in revenues from taxes on specific goods and services but decreases in those from general taxes on goods and services as well as other tax types. The Philippines' increase in tax revenue was mainly due to taxes on income, profits and capital gains and social security contributions. For Korea, large increases in revenues from taxes on income, profits and capital gains as well as other taxes cancelled out decreases in revenues from general taxes on goods and services, resulting in a net increase of 0.7 p.p.

Figure 1.3. **Annual changes in tax-to-GDP ratios (p.p.), 2015**

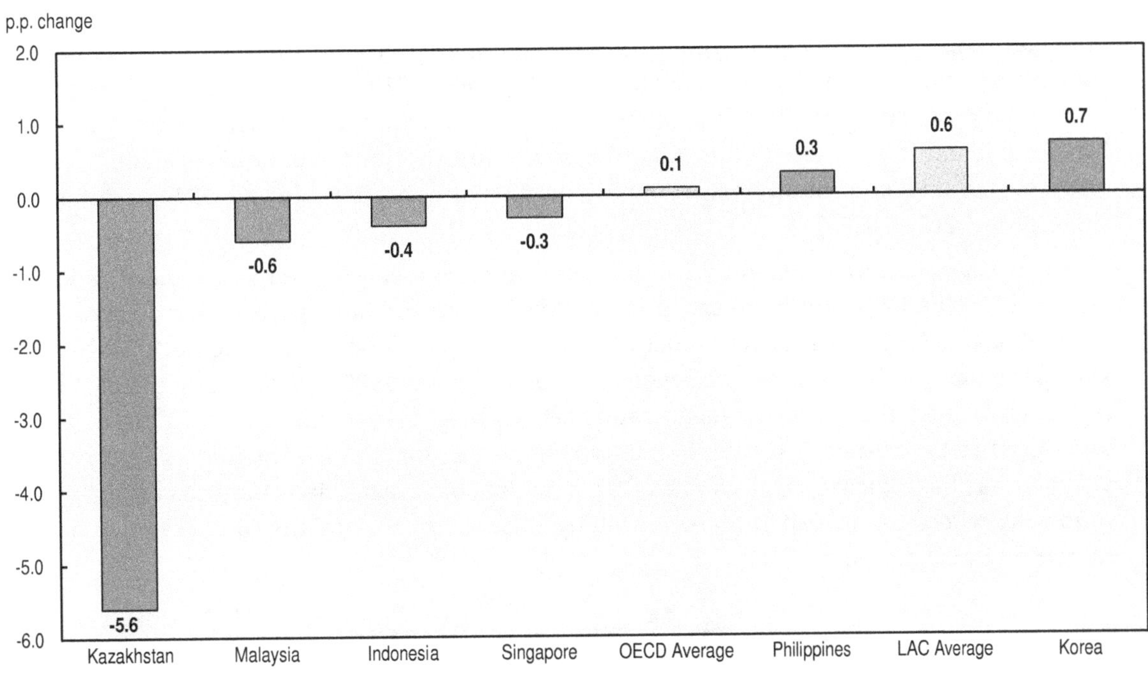

Note: Data for Korea, Japan and the OECD average are taken from *Revenue Statistics* (OECD, 2016a) and are preliminary for 2015, except for Japan, where some 2015 data are not available.

Source: Authors' calculations based on Table 3.1.

StatLink *http://dx.doi.org/10.1787/888933543334*

Figure 1.4. **Net changes in tax-to-GDP ratios between 2014 and 2015 by main type of taxes (p.p.)**

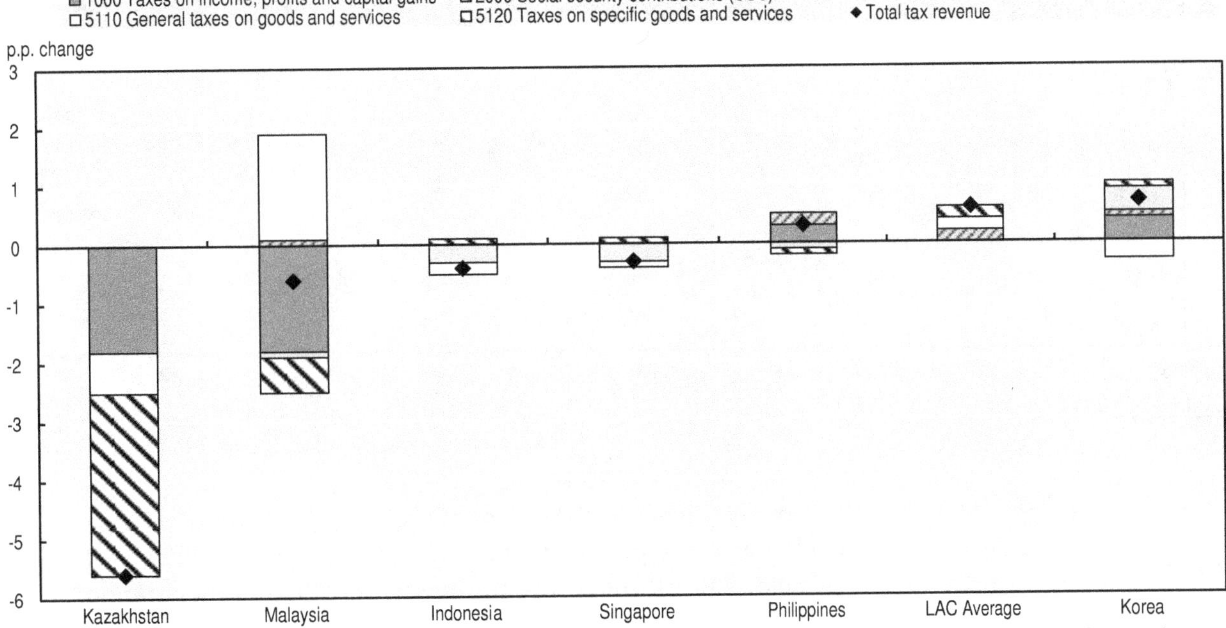

Note: Data for Korea, Japan and the OECD average are taken from *Revenue Statistics* (OECD, 2016a) and are preliminary for 2015 in Korea. Data for 2014 is used for the OECD average and for Japan as data for 2015 are not available.

Source: Authors' calculations based on tables in Chapter 3.

StatLink *http://dx.doi.org/10.1787/888933543353*

The tax-to-GDP ratio is affected by broader macroeconomic conditions. Asia as a whole continues to suffer from the slow recovery of developed countries from the financial crisis, the fall of commodity prices and a number of trade protectionist measures that hinder the rise in exports (UNESCAP, 2014). OECD (2016b) explains that "recent external shocks that are affecting economic activity in the region include (…) China's further economic slowdown". For example, lower international demand for goods and services, reduced commodity prices, and lower investment have slowed GDP growth in Indonesia (OECD, 2015a).

The Asian countries featured in this publication increased their tax-to-GDP ratios between 2000 and 2015, with the exception of Kazakhstan and Singapore, which decreased by 4.3 p.p. and 1.9 p.p. respectively over this period. This is illustrated in Figure 1.5, which shows the tax-to-GDP ratios for the seven countries between 1990 and 2015. Since 2003, the rate of growth for the Southeast Asian countries has been slower than the Latin American and Caribbean countries (LAC) average. Over that period, the LAC average increased by 4.8 p.p. whereas the increase was less than 1.3 p.p. in the Southeast Asian countries except for Indonesia whose tax-to-GDP ratio increased by 3.2 p.p.. In contrast, the OECD average has increased by 0.3 p.p. since 2000.

Figure 1.5. **Tax-to-GDP ratios (%), 1990-2015**

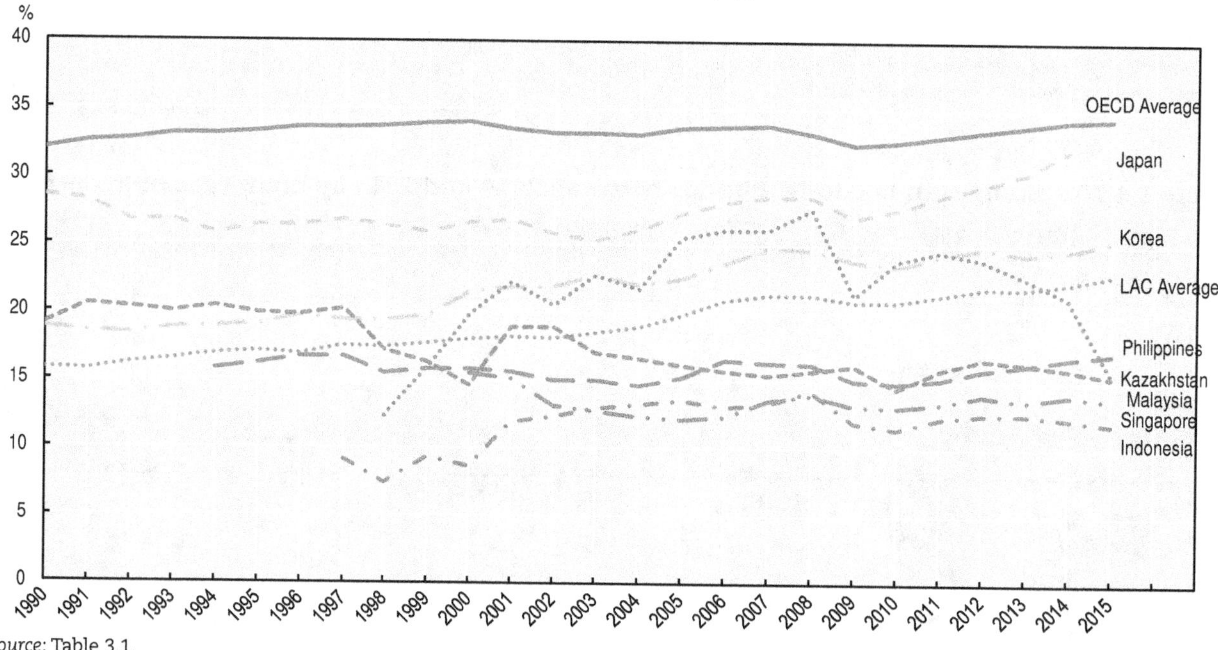

Source: Table 3.1.

StatLink http://dx.doi.org/10.1787/888933543372

Between 2000 and 2015, increases in tax-to-GDP ratios of over 3.0 p.p. occurred in Korea and Indonesia. In that period Indonesia improved its revenue collection and the efficiency of its tax administration (Arnold, 2012) through the introduction of tax administration reforms in the 2000s, particularly with respect to personal income taxes (OECD, 2015a). One key reform was the creation of offices targeted at specific taxpayer groups such as the high-wealth individual, medium and small taxpayer offices (OECD, 2015b).

Malaysia and the Philippines had increases of 0.7 p.p. and 1.2 p.p., respectively, between 2000 and 2015. The Philippines have modernised their tax administration to increase taxpayer compliance and to improve collection efficiency (for example, the introduction of electronic tax services (e.g. eFPS) and mandatory use of such system). In addition major efforts were made to increase the number of taxpayers, resulting in an increase of 71% between 2007 and 2013. However, this has not resulted in a significant increase in tax revenues because of limited tax bases and high evasion (OECD, 2015b).

The financial crisis affected the tax-to-GDP ratios for the Asian countries featured in this publication. All seven countries experienced decreases between 2008 and 2010, ranging from -0.9 p.p. in Singapore to -3.8 p.p. in Kazakhstan. Following the crisis, the tax-to-GDP ratios in all countries have increased back toward pre-crisis levels except in Indonesia and Kazakhstan.

Revenues from each tax category as percentage of GDP decreased in Indonesia, with corporate income tax and VAT revenues most affected over this period. This was due to the impacts of declining GDP growth on tax revenue and the reduction of income tax rates in 2009 as part of a stimulus package that also included the removal of some tax and import duties. Under this package the top personal income tax rate was reduced from 35% to 30% and the corporate income tax rate from 30% to 28% (Basri and Rahardja, 2011).

Factors influencing tax-to-GDP ratios

Tax-to-GDP ratios are influenced by a variety of domestic and international factors. Domestically, macroeconomic characteristics such as the importance of agriculture in the economy, resource endowments, openness to trade and the size of the informal economy can influence tax-to-GDP ratios. The power of tax administrations, the levels of corruption and tax morale (or willingness of people to pay taxes) are also strongly linked to the level of tax revenues (OECD, 2014). Aizenman et al (2015) found that in Asia, government effectiveness and institution quality are positively correlated with the level of tax-to-GDP ratio. Geographic location is also relevant: landlocked countries are less able to impose taxes on goods and services entering the country than island countries (UNESCAP, 2014). In addition, international factors, including the tax policies of other countries, can impact tax-to-GDP ratios.

Higher shares of agriculture in GDP are associated with lower tax-to-GDP ratios (Gupta, 2015; Addison and Levin, 2012; Profeta and Scabrosetti, 2010). This finding is mirrored in the revenue data for most of the Asian countries featured in the publication, where countries with higher shares of agriculture display lower tax-to-GDP ratios. Agriculture amounts to more than 8% of GDP in Indonesia, Malaysia and the Philippines and their tax-to-GDP ratios are all below 18%. In contrast, agriculture is less than 3% of GDP in Japan and Korea and their tax ratios are above 25% (Japan's tax-to-GDP ratio refers to 2014 as 2015 data are not available). However, in Singapore, the agricultural sector is very small as a share of GDP, but the tax-to-GDP ratio is relatively low.

The inverse relationship between agriculture and tax revenues as a percentage of GDP is explained by several factors. Firstly, agriculture is a challenging sector to tax: most people in this sector in developing economies are on low incomes and many are not registered for tax purposes (EPS PEAKS, 2013). Secondly, agriculture benefits from numerous tax exemptions. For example, Malaysia allows an agriculture allowance to be deducted from profits of eligible businesses (Inland Revenue Board of Malaysia, 2016) and goods and services related to the agriculture sector are exempt from import duty, sales tax and excise duty (Ministry of International Trade and Industry, 2016).

Figure 1.6. **Agriculture as % of GDP and tax-to-GDP ratios, 2015**

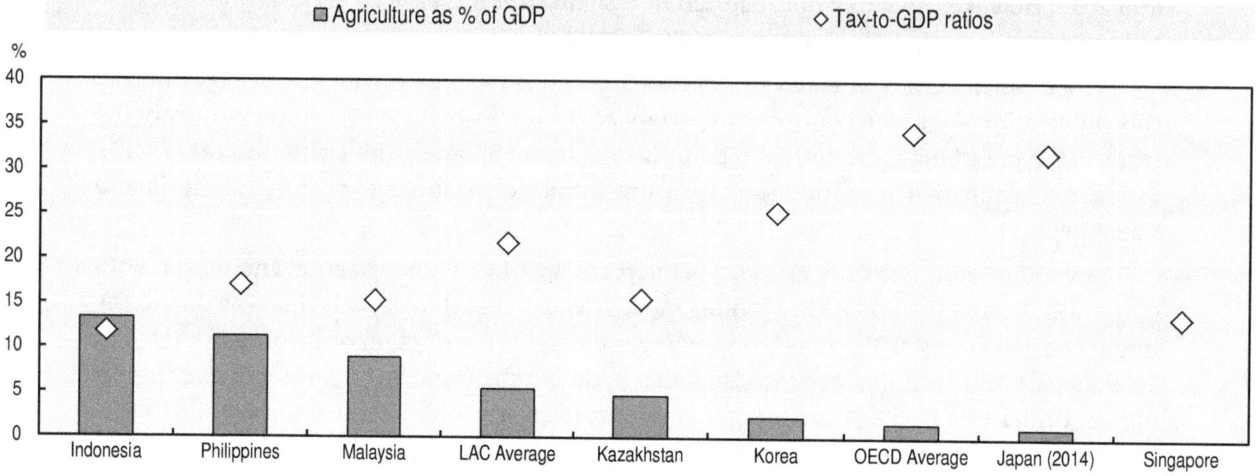

Note: The indicator agriculture as % of GDP includes forestry, hunting and fishing, as well as cultivation of crops and livestock production. The LAC average includes developing Latin American and Caribbean countries only. The latest data for the agriculture as % of GDP are for 2014. Data for Korea, Japan and the OECD average are taken from *Revenue Statistics* (OECD, 2016a) and are preliminary for 2015 in Korea. Data for 2014 are used for Japan as data for 2015 are not available.

Source: World Bank for the figures on agriculture as % of GDP. Table 3.1 for the tax-to-GDP ratios.

StatLink ⟶ *http://dx.doi.org/10.1787/888933543391*

Tax exemptions and incentives can reduce the levels of tax ratios. As Southeast Asian countries have increasingly integrated into the global market they have reduced corporate income tax rates and import tariffs, in line with the international trends. The countries have also developed broad tax-incentive schemes to encourage foreign investment. Tax incentive schemes have put pressure on corporate income tax revenues, particularly following ASEAN[2] integration. In 2007, as part of the ASEAN integration, the ASEAN economies endorsed the Economic Community blueprint "to establish ASEAN as a single market and production base making ASEAN more dynamic and competitive with new mechanisms and measures to strengthen the implementation of its existing economic initiatives" (ASEAN, 2008). UNESCAP (2016) explains that "since the adoption of the ASEAN Economic Community blueprint in 2007, several countries have further reduced their CIT rate and expanded tax incentives and exemptions for investors".

Changes in tax-to-GDP ratios from 2000-15 by tax category

Changes in the overall tax-to-GDP ratios between 2000 and 2015 in the seven countries were caused by a variety of changes in the categories of tax revenues. The biggest changes to a category of tax revenue over this period occurred in taxes on incomes and profits as percentage of GDP (where Malaysia showed an increase of 1.4 p.p.) and in social security contributions (where Japan and Korea saw an increase of over 3 p.p.). Changes in each of the subcategories are shown in Figure 1.7.

Figure 1.7. Changes in tax-to-GDP ratios by type of taxes between 2000 and 2015 (p.p.)

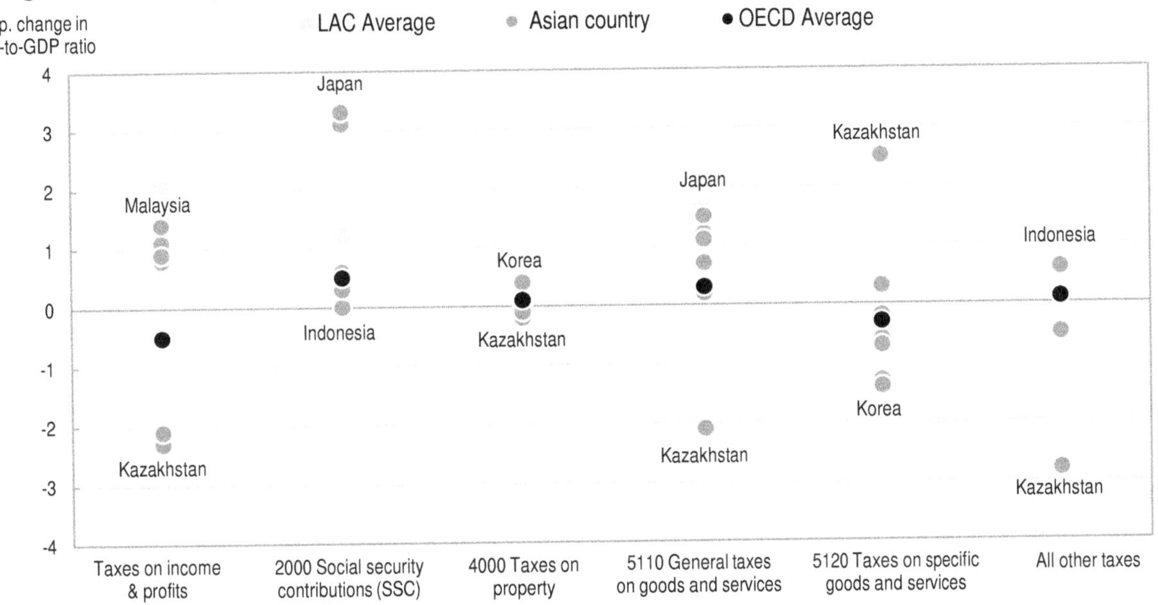

Note: Data for Korea, Japan and the OECD average are taken from *Revenue Statistics* (OECD, 2016a) and are preliminary for 2015. Data for the OECD average and for Japan refer to 2000-14 as some data for 2015 are not available.

Source: Authors' calculations based on tables in Chapter 3.

StatLink ⟶ http://dx.doi.org/10.1787/888933543410

In Malaysia and the Philippines, the growth of the tax-to-GDP ratio from 2000 to 2015 is primarily due to increases in taxes on incomes and profits. In Japan and Korea, the predominant driver of growth (as a percentage of GDP) is the increase in social security contributions whereas in Indonesia, increases were seen across different categories, with the biggest increase in revenues from taxes on general goods and services. In Kazakhstan, negative growth of the tax-to-GDP ratio is due to decreases in revenues from taxes on income and profits and other taxes which have decreased respectively by 2.3 p.p. and 2.9 p.p. (the decrease in other taxes is explained entirely by a decrease in payroll tax revenues). The tax-to-GDP ratio in Singapore is lower in 2015 relative to 2000, driven by the decrease of individual income tax rates and corporate income tax rates. The change in tax revenues in each category (as a percentage of GDP) between 2000 and 2015 is depicted in Figure 1.8 for each country.

The growth of revenue from taxes on incomes and profits as a percentage of GDP in Malaysia and Philippines is consistent with the broader trend for developing countries. As countries increase their level of development they tend to collect more of their tax revenue from taxes on incomes and profits relative to taxes on goods and services (UNESCAP, 2014).

Another contributor to the higher revenues in Malaysia was changes to the tax administration. The most important were providing more autonomy by making the tax administration into a statutory authority in 1996; a change in the tax collection from formal to self-assessment (2000-04); and deployment of more of the workforce to compliance programmes and enforcement tasks. As with many countries both outside and inside the OECD, income tax revenues in Malaysia decreased following the financial crisis, by over 1 p.p. in 2010. However the subsequent increase in 2011 returned the tax-to-GDP ratio to above the pre-crisis levels. This was partially a reflection of further changes to working practices and the organisation of the tax administration that improved the efficiency of the tax collection process (OECD, 2015b).

Figure 1.8. **Net changes in tax-to-GDP ratios between 2000 and 2015 by main type of taxes (p.p.)**

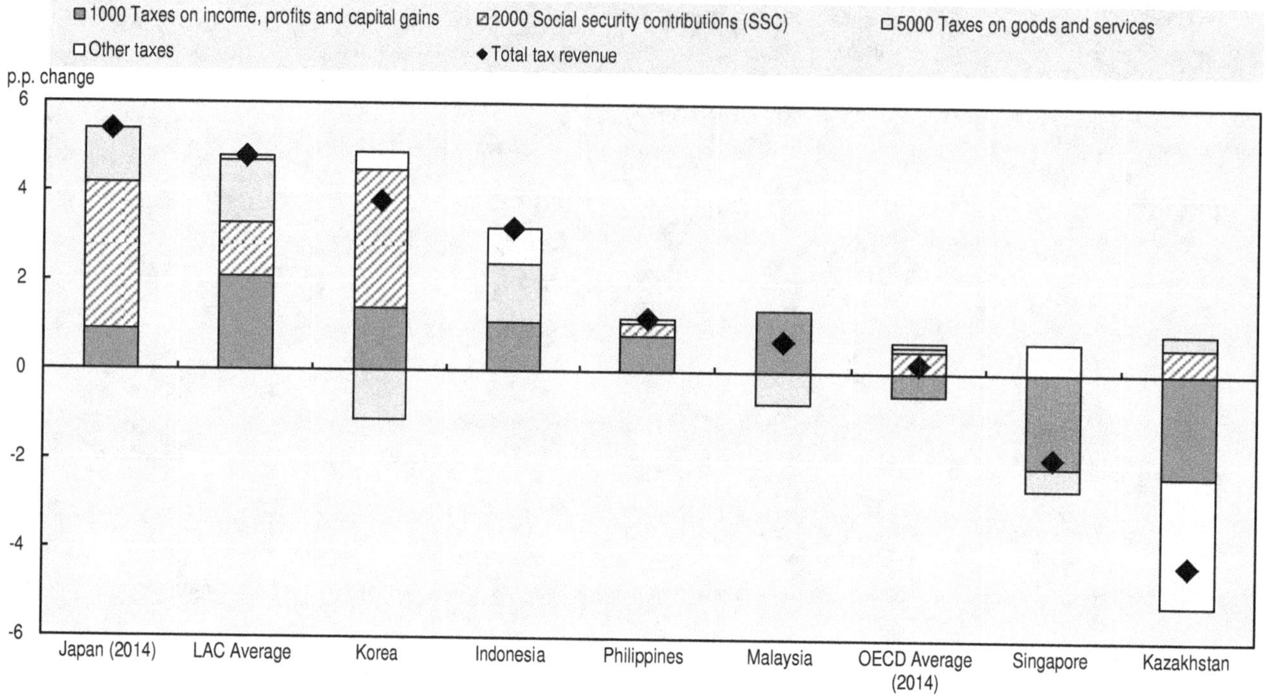

Note: Data for Korea, Japan and the OECD average are taken from *Revenue Statistics* (OECD, 2016a) and are preliminary for 2015 in Korea. Data for 2014 are used for the OECD average and for Japan as data for 2015 are not available.
Source: Authors' calculations based on tables in Chapter 3.

StatLink *http://dx.doi.org/10.1787/888933543429*

In Japan and Korea, social security contributions were the main contributors to the increase in tax revenue as percentage of GDP since 2000. The increase in social security contributions in Japan and Korea accounted for more than 3 p.p. of GDP in each country, as shown in Figure 1.8. In Japan, the change resulted from reforms in 2000, 2004 and 2009 to secure the sustainability of social security systems in light of an ageing population. These reforms included increases to premiums and the pensionable age (SSA, 2000; IPSS, 2014).

Japan and Korea have the highest revenues from social security contributions among the seven countries as a percentage of GDP.[3] Social security contributions in Japan and Korea stood respectively at 12.7% and 6.7% of GDP whereas they represented less than 2.5% of GDP in Indonesia, Kazakhstan, Malaysia and the Philippines (Figure 1.9). The range of social security contributions as a percentage of GDP reflects the wide divergence of social security systems and the instruments used to deliver social protection in Asia. For example, in Indonesia, social protection takes the form of social assistance (non-contributory) rather than a social security system (contributory). Social security contributions are therefore negligible and relate only to the "Asuransi Kesehatan" – a health insurance programme for employees in for-profit state-owned enterprises. In Malaysia, civil servants are not required to contribute to their pensions, which are partially financed from the government budget (Bauer and Thant, 2010).

Figure 1.9. **Tax revenue by main type of taxes as % of GDP, 2015**

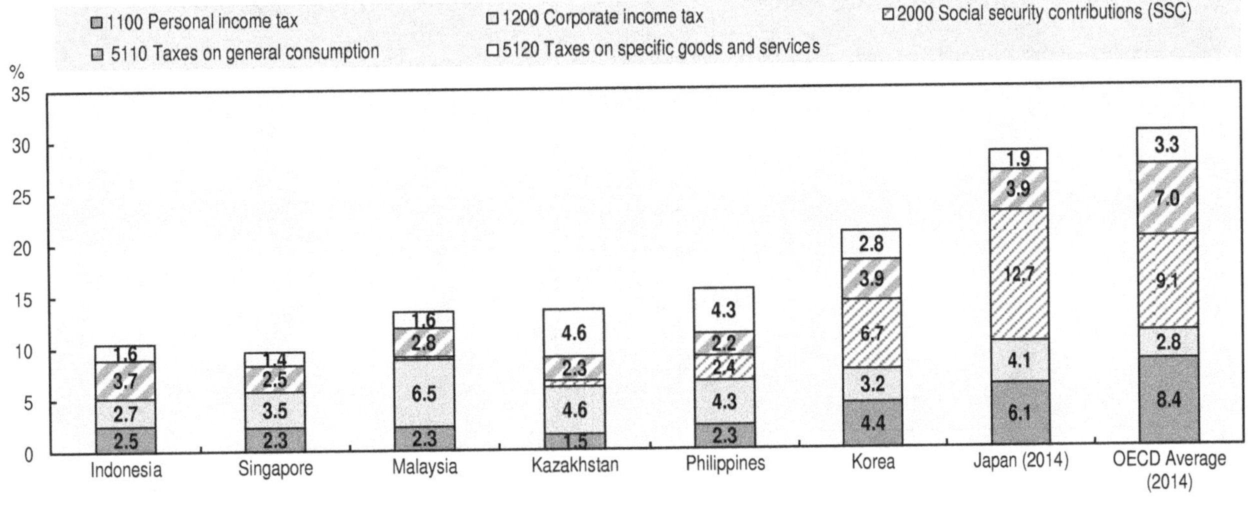

Note: Less than 5% of revenue from taxes on income and profits cannot be allocated to corporate income tax revenue or personal income tax revenue in Malaysia, the Philippines and Singapore. Data for Korea, Japan and the OECD average are taken from *Revenue Statistics* (OECD, 2016a) and are preliminary for 2015 in Korea. Data for 2014 are used for the OECD average and for Japan as data for 2015 are not available.

Source: Tables in Chapter 3.

StatLink *http://dx.doi.org/10.1787/888933543448*

Corporate income taxes are a significant source of tax revenue in each of the countries in this publication. The share of corporate income tax revenues-to-GDP is higher than the OECD average in all countries except Indonesia, ranging from 2.7% of GDP in Indonesia to 6.5% in Malaysia in 2015, compared to the OECD average of 2.8% in 2014 (data in 2015 are not available). Corporate income tax revenue as a percentage of GDP in Malaysia is significantly more than that of the other countries, which is partly explained by revenue derived from petroleum companies which are taxed at a higher rate (38%) than the standard corporate tax rate (25%) (Oxford Business Group, 2014). Revenues from petroleum companies represented about 1.0% of GDP in 2015.

Between 2000 and 2015, corporate income tax rates were reduced in each of the seven countries, although corporate income tax revenues as a percentage of GDP in 2015 remained at the same level or increased compared to 2000, with the exception of Indonesia, Kazakhstan and Singapore. Corporate income tax revenues in Indonesia began decreasing as a percentage of GDP in 2008, following the first of two decreases in the corporate income tax rate (Figures 1.10 and 1.11). In Kazakhstan, corporate income tax revenue as a percentage of GDP increased up to 2008 to reach its peak at 13.4% and decreased steadily to reach its lowest level in 2015 at 4.6%. The decreases were partly driven by the sharp decrease in the rate from 30% to 20% in 2009 (Figure 1.12 and 1.13). In Singapore, the fall in corporate income tax revenues as a percentage of GDP coincided with the gradual decrease in corporate tax rates from 26% in 2000 to 17% in 2015 (Figure 1.14 and 1.15).

Personal income tax revenues in the seven countries are lower as a percentage of GDP than the OECD average. Two factors contribute to these lower levels. Firstly, a larger population of taxpayers are on low incomes and are exempt from paying taxes. Secondly, personal income tax revenue may be reduced by non-compliance and tax evasion of some high-income individuals. As a result, in many Asian countries, a small proportion of the population bears the tax burden (UNESCAP, 2014).

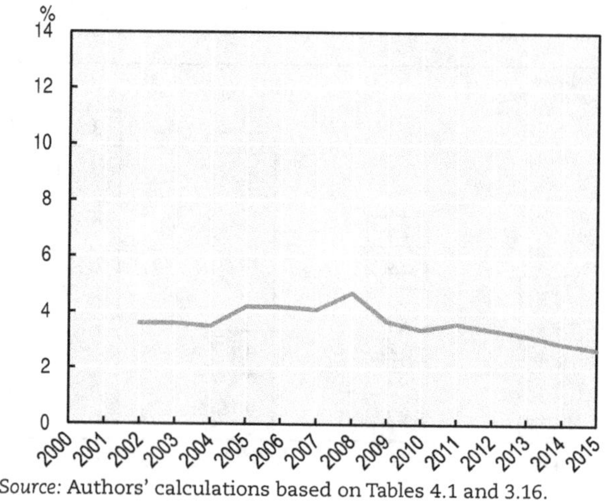

Figure 1.10. **Corporate income tax revenue as % of GDP in Indonesia, 2000-15**

Source: Authors' calculations based on Tables 4.1 and 3.16.

StatLink ᐈ *http://dx.doi.org/10.1787/888933543467*

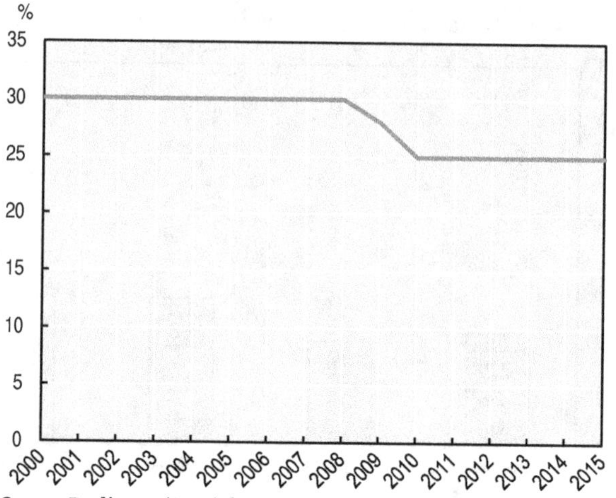

Figure 1.11. **Corporate income tax rates in Indonesia, 2000-15**

Source: Berlianto (2009) for corporate income tax rates up to 2005, KPMG (2016) for corporate income tax rates for 2006-15.

StatLink ᐈ *http://dx.doi.org/10.1787/888933543486*

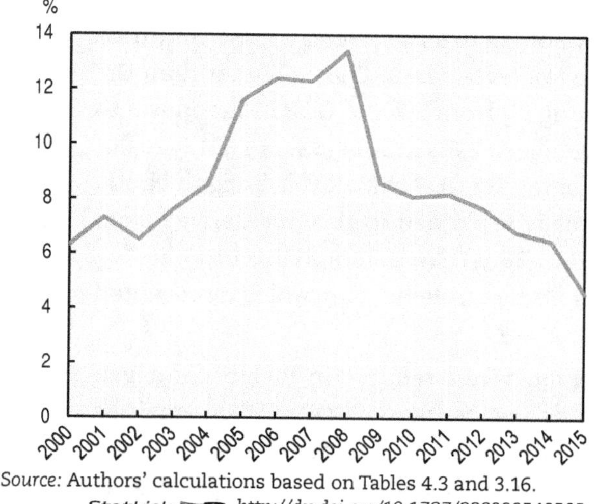

Figure 1.12. **Corporate income tax revenue as % of GDP in Kazakhstan, 2000-15**

Source: Authors' calculations based on Tables 4.3 and 3.16.

StatLink ᐈ *http://dx.doi.org/10.1787/888933543505*

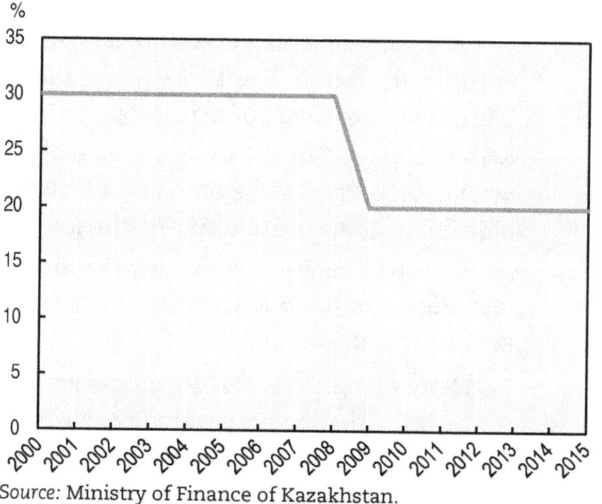

Figure 1.13. **Corporate income tax rates in Kazakhstan, 2000-15**

Source: Ministry of Finance of Kazakhstan.

StatLink ᐈ *http://dx.doi.org/10.1787/888933543524*

For example, in Indonesia, 3% of households paid more than 80% of personal tax revenues in 2010 (Nugraha and Lewis, 2011). Higher- and middle-income households in Indonesia may underreport their taxable personal income (Arnold, 2012) and the self-employed are not covered by a withholding system, so it is difficult to assess their taxable income. Indonesia has since taken measures to improve the registration of taxpayers and the number of individual taxpayers increased from 3.25 million in 2006 to almost 17 million in 2010 (Arnold, 2012).

Figure 1.14. **Corporate income tax revenue as % of GDP in Singapore, 2000-15**

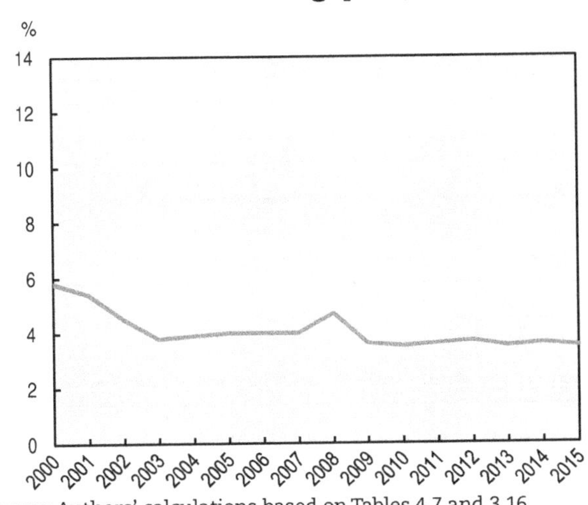

Source: Authors' calculations based on Tables 4.7 and 3.16.
StatLink ⧉ http://dx.doi.org/10.1787/888933543543

Figure 1.15. **Corporate income tax rates in Singapore, 2000-15**

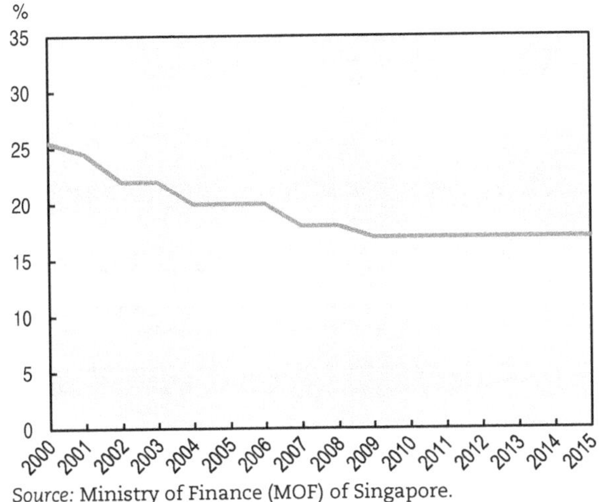

Source: Ministry of Finance (MOF) of Singapore.
StatLink ⧉ http://dx.doi.org/10.1787/888933543562

1.2. Tax structures

The tax structure, measured as the composition of tax revenues of different types, is a second important indicator, since different taxes have different economic and social effects. Across the seven countries in this publication, the composition of taxes varies widely, reflecting their different policy choices, economic structures and conditions, tax administration capabilities and historical factors.

Tax structures in 2015 and evolution since 2000

There is a wide divergence of tax structures across the seven countries in this publication. The countries can be divided into two main groups:

- The four Southeast Asian countries and Kazakhstan rely principally on taxes on goods and services and taxes on incomes and profits, which together make up more than 75% of total tax revenue in these countries. Within this group, the share of taxes on income and profits and on taxes on goods and services is roughly the same (around 35-45%) in Indonesia, Kazakhstan, the Philippines and Singapore whereas revenue from taxes on income and profits in Malaysia generates nearly 60% of total tax revenue.

- In contrast, the tax structures of Japan and Korea are more evenly split between the main categories of tax revenues: in Korea, tax revenue is divided roughly equally into three parts: 30.3% from taxes on income and profits, 26.6% from social security contributions, and 28% from taxes on goods and services. This tax structure is similar to the OECD average. In Japan, social security contributions amount to nearly 40% of total tax revenue and the share of taxes on goods and services was slightly below 20% in 2014.

Between 2000 and 2015, Indonesia, Japan, Malaysia and the Philippines decreased their reliance on revenues from taxes on specific goods and services (mainly excises and import and customs duties) and increased revenues from taxes on general consumption, most notably VAT (Figures 1.17 and 1.18). In contrast, Korea, Kazakhstan and Singapore decreased their reliance on taxes on general consumption and increased their reliance on taxes on specific goods and services.

Figure 1.16. **Tax structures (as % of total tax revenue), 2015**

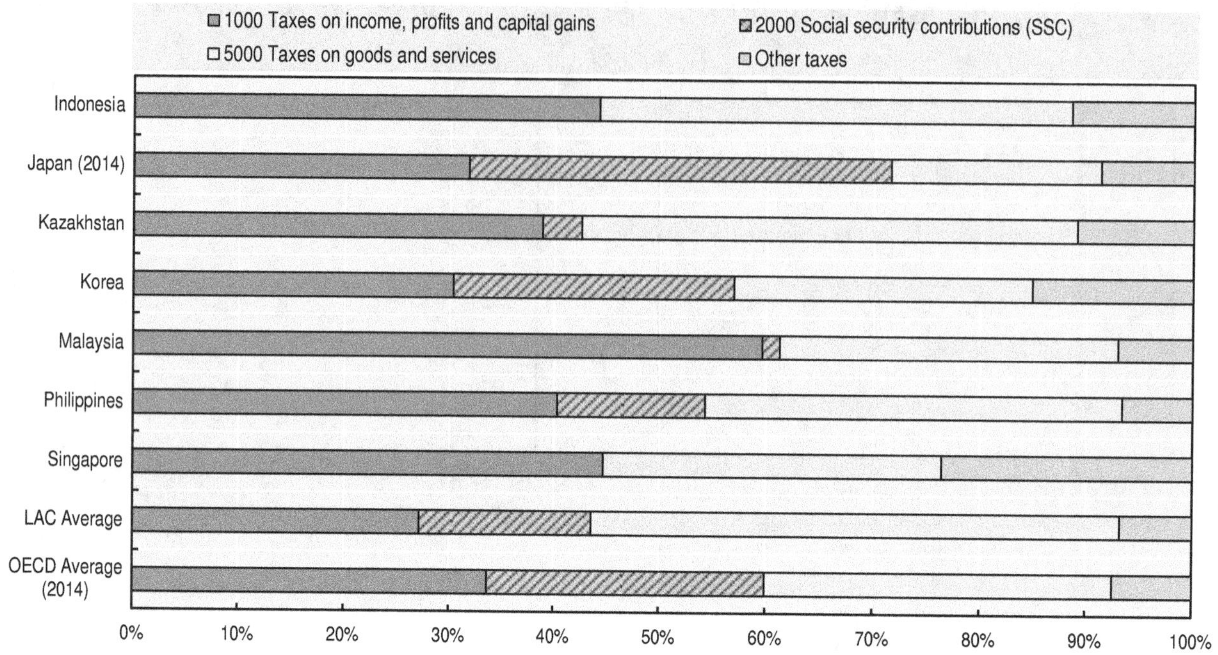

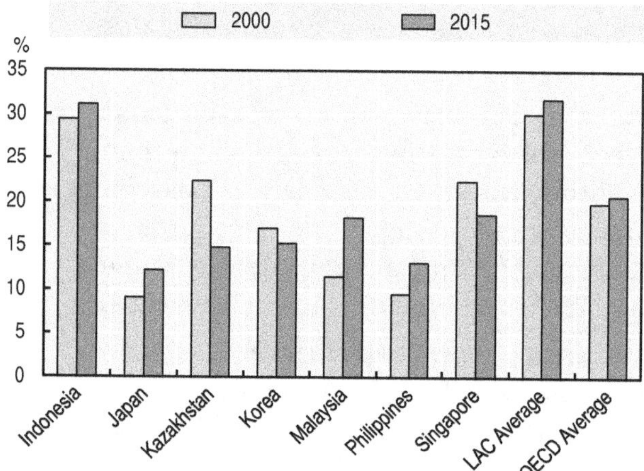

Note: Data for Korea, Japan and the OECD average are taken from *Revenue Statistics* (OECD, 2016a) and are preliminary for 2015 in Korea. Data for 2014 are used for the OECD average and for Japan as data for 2015 are not available.

Source: Authors' calculations based on tables in Chapter 4.

StatLink ᔖᔑᕝ *http://dx.doi.org/10.1787/888933543581*

Figure 1.17. **Revenue from taxes on general consumption as % of total tax revenue, 2000 and 2015**

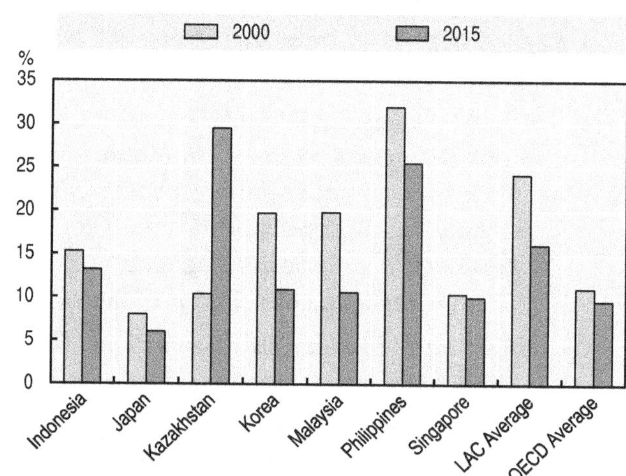

Note: Data for Korea, Japan and the OECD average are taken from *Revenue Statistics* (OECD, 2016a) and are preliminary for 2015 in Korea. Data for 2014 are used for the OECD average and for Japan as data for 2015 are not available.
Source: Table 3.13.

StatLink ᔖᔑᕝ *http://dx.doi.org/10.1787/888933543600*

Figure 1.18. **Revenue from taxes on specific goods and services as % of total tax revenue, 2000 and 2015**

Note: Data for Korea, Japan and the OECD average are taken from *Revenue Statistics* (OECD, 2016a) and are preliminary for 2015 in Korea. Data for 2014 are used for the OECD average and for Japan as data for 2015 are not available.
Source: Table 3.15.

StatLink ᔖᔑᕝ *http://dx.doi.org/10.1787/888933543619*

Over the past decades, tax revenues from import duties have decreased in many countries, partly due to trade liberalisation that took the form of reductions of tariffs and new trade agreements (UNESCAP, 2014). Since 2000, dozens of bilateral and regional trade agreements have been signed by East Asian countries (Pomfret and Sourdin, 2011). In January 2007, the ASEAN countries agreed that tariffs on all intra-ASEAN goods would be eliminated by 2015 (Safuan, 2012).

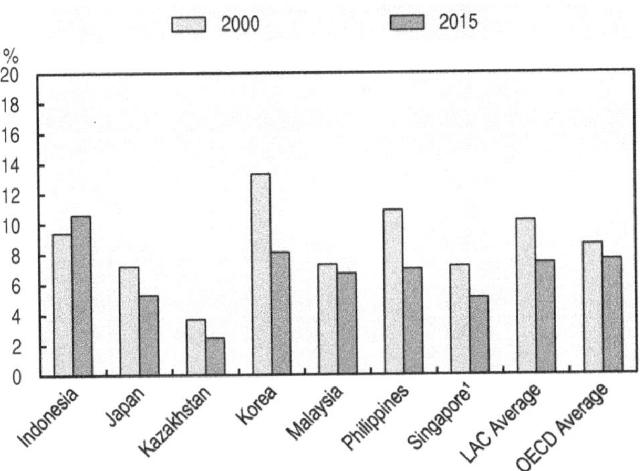

Figure 1.19. **Revenue from excises as % of total tax revenue, 2000 and 2015**

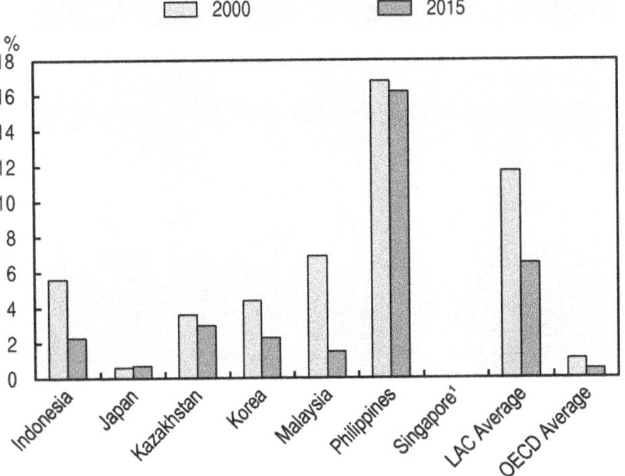

Figure 1.20. **Revenue from customs and import duties as % of total tax revenue, 2000 and 2015**

Note: Data for Korea, Japan and the OECD average are taken from *Revenue Statistics* (OECD, 2016a) and are preliminary for 2015 in Korea. Data for 2014 are used for the OECD average and for Japan as data for 2015 are not available.
1. Customs and import duties cannot be separated from excises in Singapore and have been classified in category 5121 excises.
Source: Authors' calculations based on tables in Chapter 4.

StatLink ⟐ *http://dx.doi.org/10.1787/888933543638*

Note: Data for Korea, Japan and the OECD average are taken from *Revenue Statistics* (OECD, 2016a) and are preliminary for 2015 in Korea. Data for 2014 are used for the OECD average and for Japan as data for 2015 are not available.
1. Customs and import duties cannot be separated from excises in Singapore and have been classified in category 5121 excises.
Source: Authors' calculations based on tables in Chapter 4.

StatLink ⟐ *http://dx.doi.org/10.1787/888933543657*

In Indonesia, Kazakhstan, Korea, Malaysia and the Philippines, the share of import duties[4] decreased between 2000 and 2015, consistent with these broader trends. As in OECD countries on average, the share of excises decreased in all seven countries except in Indonesia where it increased slightly over that period.

Between 2000 and 2015, the contribution of VAT to total tax revenues increased significantly in most Asian countries, including five of the seven countries in this publication. In Kazakhstan and Korea, revenues from VAT as percentage of total tax revenues have decreased. In Kazakhstan, this is partly due to the steady decrease in the VAT standard rate from 20% in 2000 to 12% in 2015. All seven countries source an important part of their revenue from VAT, except for Malaysia, which introduced VAT in 2015, having relied previously on a goods and services tax. Across the seven countries, VAT revenue as a percentage of total tax revenue ranges from 13% in the Philippines to 31% in Indonesia in 2015 (Figure 1.21). The figure for the Philippines needs to be interpreted with caution as the data exclude revenue from VAT on imports that could not be distinguished from revenue from other import duties.

The share of the VAT to total tax revenues in each country remains smaller than the OECD average of 20%, except in Indonesia. This is partially due to the lower VAT rates in many Asian countries compared to OECD countries. VAT rates in the seven countries ranged from 7% in Singapore to 12% in Kazakhstan and the Philippines in 2015 (Tradingeconomics, 2016), whereas the average standard VAT rate is 19% in OECD countries (Ernst and Young, 2015).

Figure 1.21. **Revenue from VAT as % of total tax revenue, 2000 and 2015**

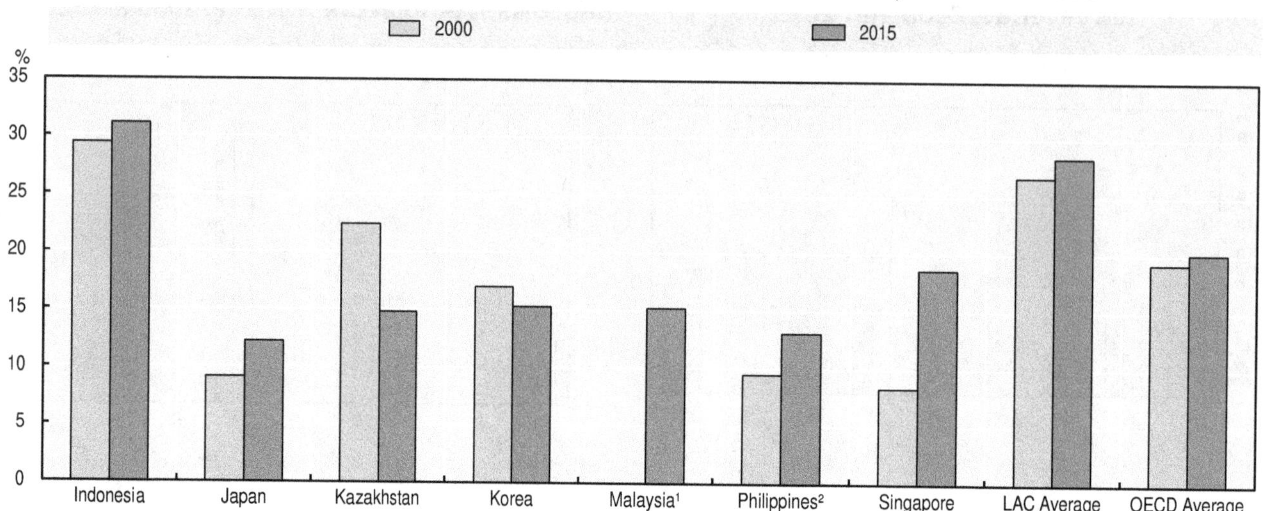

Note: Data for Korea, Japan and the OECD average are taken from *Revenue Statistics* (OECD, 2016a) and are preliminary for 2015 in Korea. Data for 2014 are used for the OECD average and for Japan as data for 2015 are not available.
1. Malaysia introduced a VAT in 2015 and previously relied on a goods and services tax until 2014.
2. The figure needs to be interpreted with caution as the data exclude revenue from VAT on imports that could not be distinguished from revenue from other import duties.
Source: Authors' calculations based on tables in Chapter 4.

StatLink *http://dx.doi.org/10.1787/888933543676*

The share of corporate income tax revenues to total tax revenue in the seven countries included in this publication is higher than the OECD average of 8.8% (2014 figure). The share of corporate income tax revenues to total tax revenue is around 13% in Japan and Korea and is higher in other countries, where corporate income tax revenues ranged from 23% of total tax revenue in Indonesia to 42.5% in Malaysia. Southeast Asian countries and Kazakhstan obtain a higher proportion of their revenue from corporate income taxes than from personal income taxes. In contrast, Japan and Korea have a higher share of personal income tax revenues compared to corporate tax revenues.

The share of personal income taxes to total revenue ranges from approximately 9.4% in Kazakhstan to 21.5% in Indonesia. When social security contributions are also considered, the two categories account for 60% of total tax revenues in Japan (2014); 44% in Korea; 28% in the Philippines; and less than 20% in the other countries.

As in OECD countries on average, property taxes and payroll taxes play a limited role in the tax revenues of Asian countries. The percentage of property tax revenue to total tax revenues varies from 8.5% to 13% in Japan, Korea and Singapore, and less than 4% in Indonesia, Kazakhstan, Malaysia and the Philippines. There are no payroll taxes in Indonesia, Japan, Malaysia, the Philippines and Singapore.

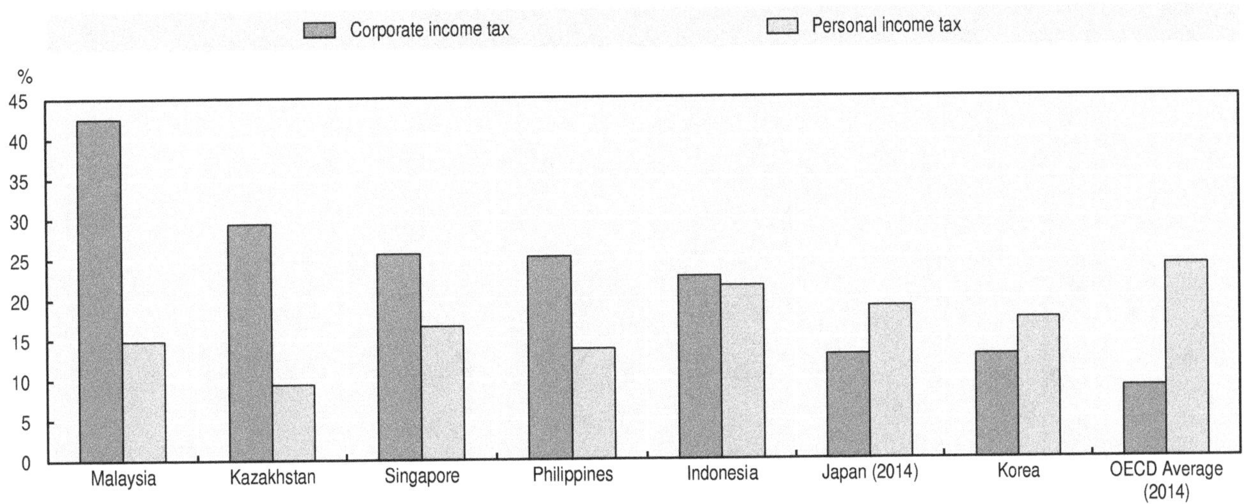

Figure 1.22. **Revenue from corporate income tax and personal income tax as % of total tax revenue, 2015**

Note: A small amount of income tax revenues (less than 5%) cannot be allocated to either personal or corporate income tax in Malaysia, the Philippines and Singapore, and is not included in this figure. Data for Korea, Japan and the OECD average are taken from *Revenue Statistics* (OECD, 2016a) and are preliminary for 2015 in Korea. Data for 2014 are used for the OECD average and for Japan as data for 2015 are not available.

Source: Authors' calculations based on tables in Chapter 4.

StatLink ᴍⁱˢᴾ *http://dx.doi.org/10.1787/888933543695*

VAT *revenue ratio*

The VAT revenue ratio (VRR) measure for Asian countries has been calculated for the first time and included in this publication. OECD (2016c) explains that "the VRR measures the difference between the VAT revenue actually collected and what would theoretically be raised if VAT was applied at the standard rate to the entire potential tax base in a "pure" VAT regime and all revenue was collected". A VRR of 100% suggests no loss of VAT revenue as a consequence of exemptions, reduced rates, fraud, evasion or tax planning. This section describes the VRR levels in the Asian countries in this publication and analyses Indonesia and the Philippines in more depth.

There was a wide disparity of VRRs in Asian countries in 2014 (Figure 1.23). The Philippines had the lowest VRR ratio at 23% and Singapore had the highest at 84%. Of the countries in this publication, Japan, Korea and Singapore have relatively high VRR (exceeding 65%), above the OECD average of 56%. This is partially because of the relatively broad VAT based in each country: Japan does not have any reduced rates and in Singapore only international services are zero-rated, with the only exemptions applying to the sales and leases of residential properties and to most financial services (MOF, 2017). Korea has a reduced rate on a number of goods and services. In comparison many OECD countries have one or more reduced rates (OECD, 2016c), which partly explains the lower average VRR in the OECD region.

Of the countries included in this publication, Indonesia had the fourth highest VRR in 2014 at 62%. This figure needs to be interpreted with caution as the VAT revenue includes revenue from the luxury tax[5] whose rates range between 10% and 125% on luxury goods (Indonesia investments, 2017). Brondolo et al. (2008) estimated that in 2001 luxury tax revenue may have represented over 10% of the VAT revenue. A decrease of 10% in VAT revenue results in the VRR decreasing by 8 p.p. from 62% to 54% in 2014.

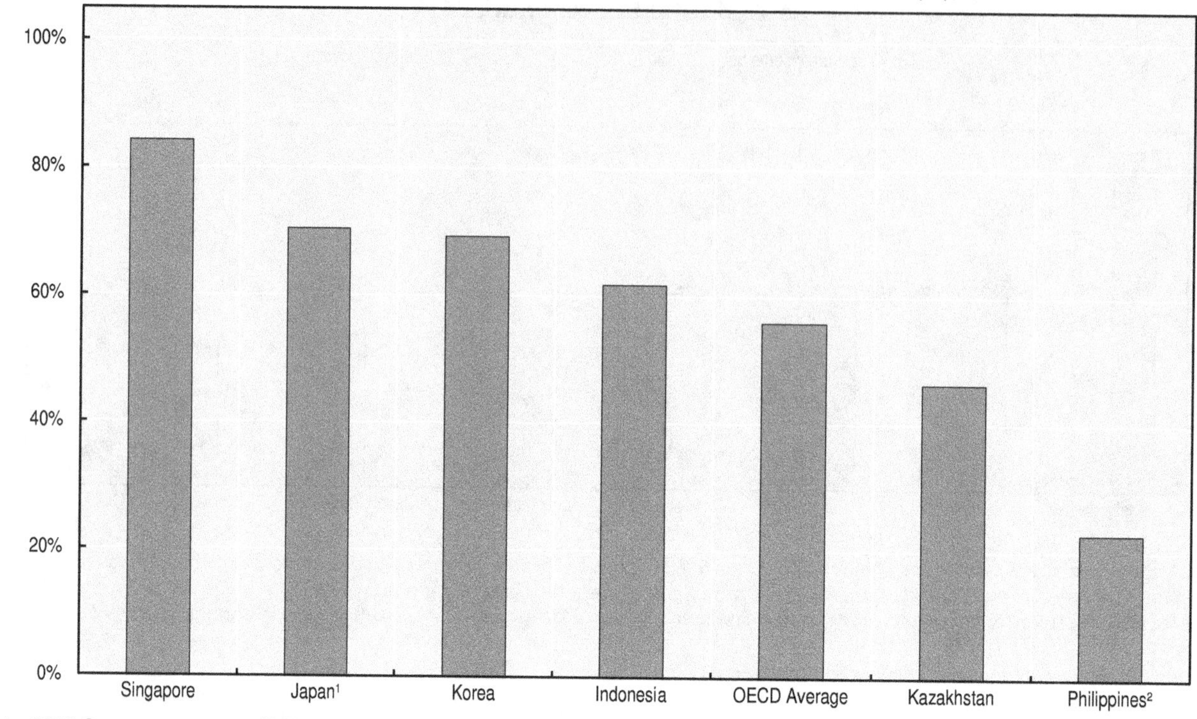
Figure 1.23. **VAT revenue ratio (VRR) in Asian countries (%), 2014**

Note: 2015 figures are not available due to missing final expenditure consumption figures for Kazakhstan, Singapore and Malaysia. Malaysia is not included as VAT was introduced in 2015.

1. Given the increase in the VAT rate from 5% to 8% on 1 April 2014, an average VAT rate was used to calculate the VRR for 2014 i.e. (5×3 + 8×9)/12 = 7.25%.

2. The VRR measure is currently underestimated as the VAT revenue collected at customs is not accounted for in total VAT revenue in this publication (this revenue could not be distinguished from revenue from other import duties and is currently classified under heading 5120 (taxes on specific goods and services)).

Source: The VAT rates are sourced from countries, Trading Economics and Deloitte websites and OECD (2016c). The final expenditure consumption figures are from the United Nations Statistics Division website and the OECD Annual National Accounts. The VAT revenues are sourced from the country tables in Chapter 4.

StatLink ᴹˢᴾ *http://dx.doi.org/10.1787/888933543714*

Moreover, the relatively high VRR rate in Indonesia also hides a number of complexities within the VAT system. On one hand, there are many exemptions on products and services in Indonesia. These include mining and drilling products, food and beverages served in hotels and restaurants, various services including healthcare, social welfare, postal delivery, financial services, religion, education, culture and entertainment (IBFD, 2017). IMF (2017) estimated that the VAT revenue loss due to exemptions on final consumption of goods and services in Indonesia amounted to 0.8% of GDP. On the other hand, a few aspects of the design of the VAT system artificially inflate revenue and therefore the VRR. Many exemptions in Indonesia relate to intermediate consumption leading to a cascading effect that increases VAT revenue (IMF, 2017).[6] IMF (2017) estimated that this amounted to around 0.9 % of GDP. Another factor influencing the VRR in Indonesia is the VAT refunds process. IMF (2017) explains that "the refund procedure is excessively long. Regular taxpayers (…) are audited prior to receiving a refund payment". This aspect of the VAT administration may discourage taxpayers to claim their due VAT refunds resulting in higher VAT revenue and VRR.

In the Philippines, the VRR was 23% in 2014. However, this figure also needs to be interpreted with caution. The VRR measure is currently underestimated as the VAT revenue collected at customs is not included with the Philippines' total VAT revenue in this publication.[7] Using publicly available estimates of this VAT revenue (BOC, 2015), the VRR increases from 23% to 47%. However, even this adjusted VRR remains one of the lowest of the countries in this publication. The Department of Finance (DOF) has noted that VAT revenue collection is particularly low in comparison to Thailand, which collects a similar VAT share as a percentage of GDP with a lower standard rate (DOF, 2016). The DOF saw this as being due to the Philippines' tax code, "which contains 59 lines of exemptions from the Value-Added Tax and 84 special VAT-related laws, [which] have led to massive revenue leakages costing the government an estimated P90.7 billion each year (…)". The government is considering a tax reform which will rationalise the VAT system and remove some exemptions, while maintaining exemptions of senior citizens and persons with disabilities, raw food purchases and health and education expenses (DOF, 2017). This may increase VAT revenue and the VRR in the future.

Figure 1.24. VAT revenue ratio (VRR) in Asian countries (%), 1990-2014

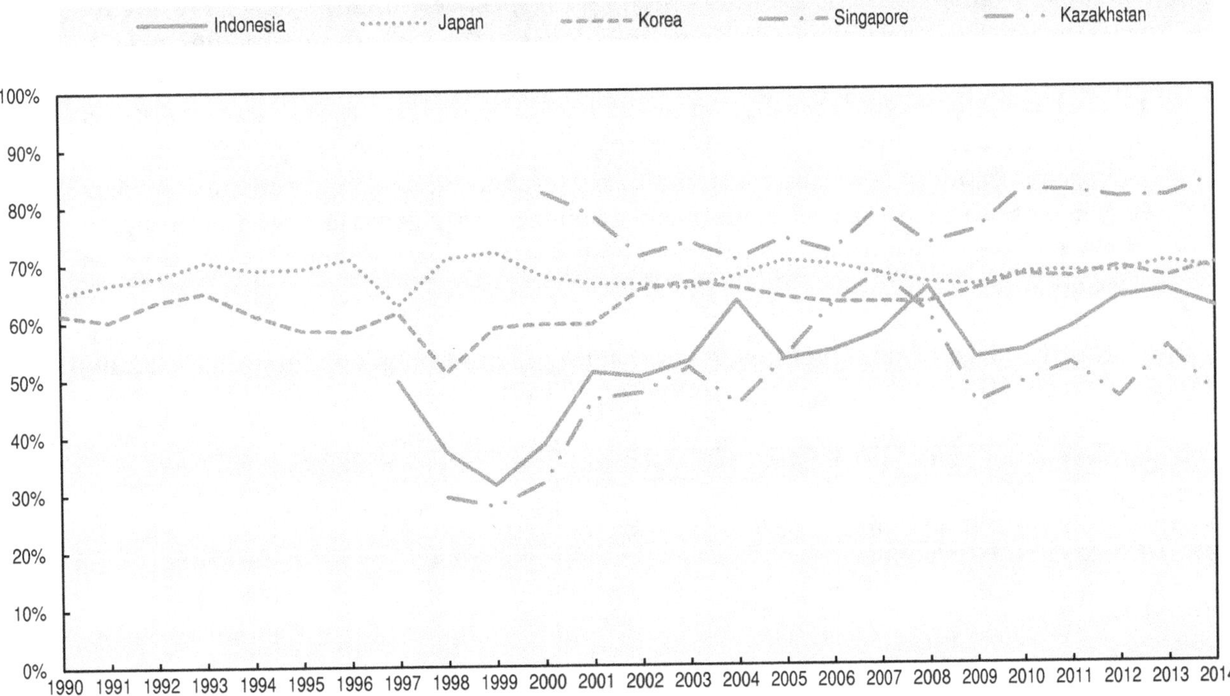

Note: 2015 figures are not available due to missing final expenditure consumption figures for Kazakhstan, Singapore and Malaysia. Malaysia is not included as VAT was introduced in 2015. The Philippines are excluded as the VRR's trend may not be representative because of the exclusion of the VAT revenue at customs in the total VAT revenue.

Source: The VAT rates are sourced from countries, Trading Economics and Deloitte websites and OECD (2016c). The final expenditure consumption figures are from the United Nations Statistics Division website and the OECD Annual National Accounts. The VAT revenues are sourced from the country tables in Chapter 4.

StatLink http://dx.doi.org/10.1787/888933543733

The VRR has not evolved greatly for Japan, Korea and Singapore since 2000 (Figure 1.24) whereas it has experienced major changes in Indonesia and Kazakhstan over that period. Looking more closely at Indonesia, its VRR has increased significantly since the late 1990s experiencing sharp declines in 2005, 2009 and 2010. Between 2000 and 2004, the VRR for Indonesia nearly doubled and increased from 38% to 63% and VAT revenue increased from 2.5% of GDP to 4.5% over that period, which coincided with the recovery from the Asian financial crisis of 1997/98 in many Asian countries. Since 2001, Indonesia has undertaken extensive tax administration reforms to improve the effectiveness and efficiency of the Department General of Taxes (DGT). These reforms aimed to make taxpayer services and enforcement programmes more effective, improve tax administration structure and update information systems (Brondolo et al., 2008). The combination of structural economic changes and the tax administration improvements accounts for the increase in VAT revenue. Following this, VAT revenues as a percentage of GDP decreased in 2005, with a further decrease between 2008 and 2010 following the global financial crisis.

1.3. Taxes by level of government

The proportion of total revenues collected by local government in Malaysia and the Philippines is relatively small at 3.3% and 5.3% respectively in 2015. Singapore, a city-state, has no local government divisions. In Indonesia, the proportion attributed to local governments is rising and was over 9% in 2015, following the shift of property taxation to the local level in 2014. Local government revenues in Japan, Kazakhstan and Korea are substantially higher at 23.4% (2014), 23.9% and 18.2% respectively. The corresponding average for OECD unitary countries was 11.7%. The share of local government revenue is high in Japan since local governments finance a wide range of goods and services including public welfare. They are also responsible for financing some education and debt services (Bessho, 2016).

Table 1.1. Attribution of tax revenues to sub-sectors of general government as % of total tax revenue, 2015

	Federal or Central government				State/Regional				Local government				Social Security Funds			
	1995	2000	2010	2015	1995	2000	2010	2015	1995	2000	2010	2015	1995	2000	2010	2015
Federal countries																
Malaysia	97.5	94.5	94.4	94.8	..	..	..	..	2.5	3.4	4.2	3.3	..	2.1	1.4	2.0
OECD[1]	52.5	55.9	53.0	53.4	16.0	15.4	16.4	16.7	7.7	6.9	8.0	7.6	23.6	21.5	22.4	22.2
Unitary countries																
Indonesia	..	96.5	92.1	91.5	..	..	..	..	..	3.5	7.0	9.3	..	..	..	..
Kazakhstan	..	50.0	81.1	72.3	..	..	..	..	..	50.0	16.4	23.9	..	..	2.5	3.9
Philippines	90.7	81.0	81.8	80.6	..	..	..	..	..	5.1	5.4	5.3	9.3	13.3	12.8	14.1
Singapore	..	100.0	100.0	100.0	..	..	..	..	..	0.0	0.0	0.0	..	0.0	0.0	0.0
Japan	41.3	38.7	33.0	36.9	..	..	..	..	25.4	26.3	25.7	23.4	33.3	35.3	40.9	39.7
Korea	69.1	67.9	59.8	55.3	..	..	..	..	18.8	14.9	16.7	18.2	12.0	16.7	23.5	26.5
OECD[2]	65.5	66.4	63.4	63.5	..	..	..	..	10.7	10.8	11.8	11.7	23.5	22.6	24.5	24.5

Note: Data for Korea, Japan and the OECD average are taken from *Revenue Statistics* (OECD, 2016a) and are preliminary for 2015 in Korea. Data for 2014 are used for the OECD average and for Japan as data for 2015 are not available.
1. Represents the unweighted average for OECD federal member countries.
2. Represents the unweighted average for OECD unitary countries.

StatLink http://dx.doi.org/10.1787/888933543828

The types of taxes levied at local government level vary between countries. Local governments in Malaysia and the Philippines have a narrow range of taxes under their jurisdiction, relying on property taxes (both countries) and taxes on income and profits (the Philippines only). Local governments in Japan and Korea raised revenue from taxes on income and profits, property taxes, taxes on goods and services, payroll (Korea only) and other taxes.

Figure 1.25. **Composition of local government tax revenue by main type of taxes, 2015**

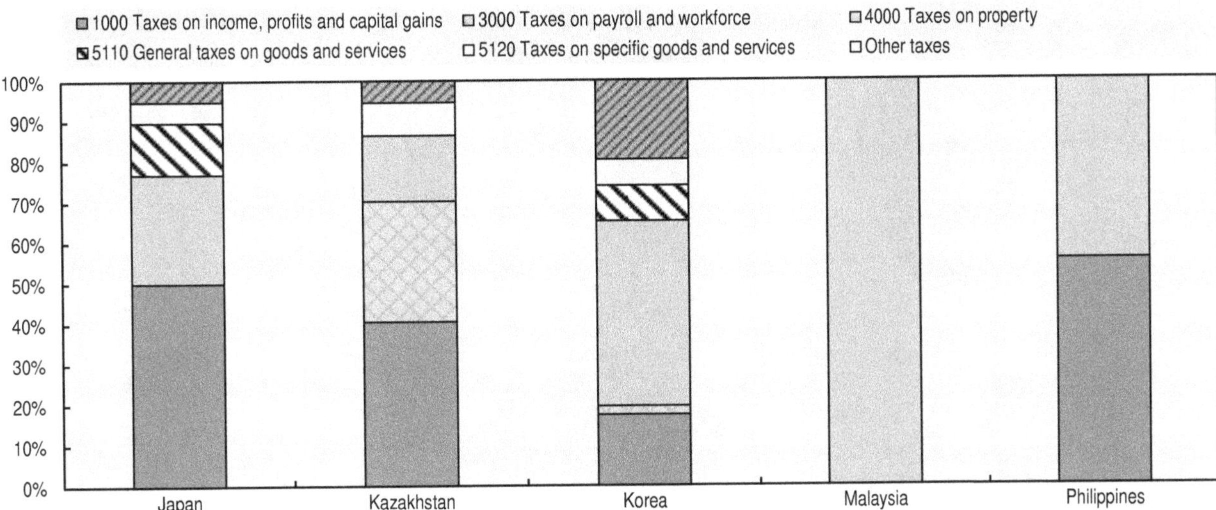

Note: Indonesia and Singapore are not included. In Indonesia, the composition of local tax revenue is unknown and is currently allocated to 6000 "Other taxes". Singapore, a city-state, has no local government divisions. Data for Korea, Japan and the OECD average are taken from *Revenue Statistics* (OECD, 2016a) and are preliminary for 2015 in Korea. Data for 2014 are used for the OECD average and for Japan as data for 2015 are not available.

Source: OECD (2017), "Revenue Statistics - Asian Countries: Comparative tables", *OECD Tax statistics* (database).

StatLink ⟐ *http://dx.doi.org/10.1787/888933543752*

Between 2000 and 2015 the share of revenues collected by local governments in Asian and OECD countries was fairly stable, with the exception of Indonesia and Kazakhstan in which the share of revenues attributed to local governments increased by 5.8 p.p. and Kazakhstan in which the share decreased by 26 p.p.

The proportion of total tax revenues collected by social security funds in Indonesia and Singapore was almost zero in 2015, whereas in the Philippines it was 14%. Tax revenues collected by social security funds in Kazakhstan and Malaysia were relatively low and amounted to 3.9% and 2.0% of total tax revenues. This compares with 39.7% in Japan (2014), 26.5% in Korea and 24.5% on average in the OECD unitary countries (2014). The share of revenues from social security funds has increased in both Japan (by 4.3 p.p.) and in Korea (9.7 p.p.) since 2000.

1.4. Comparative figures

Figure 1.26. **Tax structures, 2015**

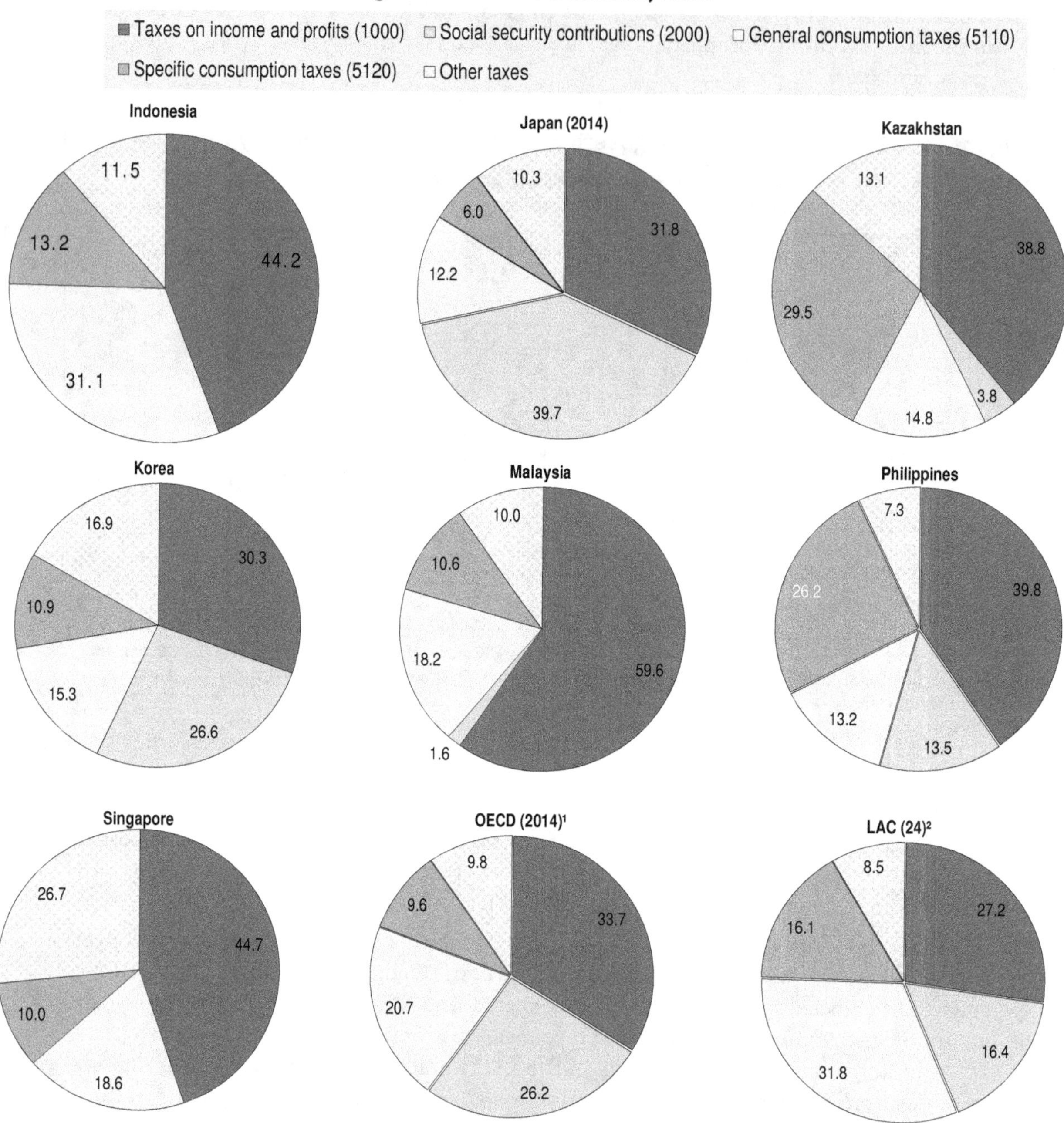

Note: Data for Korea, Japan and the OECD average are taken from *Revenue Statistics* (OECD, 2016a) and are preliminary for 2015 in Korea. Data for 2014 are used for the OECD average and for Japan as data for 2015 are not available.
1. Represents the unweighted average for OECD member countries. Japan and Korea are also part of the OECD (35) group.
2. Represents the unweighted average for 24 LAC (Latin American and Caribbean) countries.
Source: Authors' calculations based on tables in Chapter 4.

StatLink ⎙⎙ *http://dx.doi.org/10.1787/888933543771*

Notes

1. Data for Korea, Japan and the OECD average are taken from OECD (2016a), *Revenue Statistics* and are preliminary for 2015. At the time that publication was prepared, preliminary data on SSCs in 2015 for Japan were not available and consequently the tax-to-GDP ratio is not available for Japan in 2015.

2. ASEAN, the Association of Southeast Asian Nations.

3. Singapore does not levy social security contributions.

4. Customs and import duties cannot be separated from excises in Singapore and have been classified in 5111 Excises.

5. The breakdown between these two taxes is not readily available. In 2014 the luxury tax was applied to an extensive number of goods such as specified electronic appliances, housing, vehicles, alcoholic beverages, certain branded goods and household and office furnishings (PKF, 2015).

6. The cascading effect occurs when the VAT is levied on inputs used to produce VAT-exempt goods and services. In such cases, the VAT on inputs – that cannot be deducted – is transferred to the consumer through higher prices.

7. This revenue could not be distinguished from revenue from other import duties and is currently classified under heading 5120 (taxes on specific goods and services).

References

Addison, T. and J. Levin (2012), *The Determinants of Tax Revenue in Sub-Saharan Africa*, Swedish Business School at Örebro University, Örebro, Sweden, *oru.diva-portal.org/smash/record.jsf?pid=diva2%3A570456&dswid=4207*.

Aizenman, et al (2015) "Tax revenue trends in Asia and Latin America: A comparative analysis", NBER *Working Paper*, No. 21755, Cambridge, *www.nber.org/papers/w21755*.

Arnold, J. (2012), "Improving the Tax System in Indonesia", *OECD Economics Department Working Papers*, No. 998, OECD Publishing, Paris, *http://dx.doi.org/10.1787/5k912j3r2qmr-en*.

ASEAN (2008), "ASEAN Economic Community Blueprint", The Association of Southeast Asian Nations Secretariat, Jakarta, *http://asean.org/wp-content/uploads/archive/5187-10.pdf*.

Bauer, A. and M. Thant (2010), *Poverty and Sustainable Development in Asia: Impacts and Responses to the Global Economic Crisis*, ADB Publishing, Mandaluyong City, *https://www.adb.org/sites/default/files/publication/27509/poverty-sustainable-development-asia.pdf*.

Basri, M.C. and S. Rahardja (2011), "Mild Crisis, Half Hearted Fiscal Stimulus: Indonesia During the GFC", in Ito, T. and F. Parulian (eds.), "Assessment on the Impact of Stimulus, Fiscal Transparency and Fiscal Risk", *ERIA Research Project Report* 2010-01, pp.169-211, ERIA, *www.eria.org/publications/research_projectreports/images/pdf/y2010/no1/ch5Basri_andRahardjaIndonesia.pdf*.

Berlianto, A. (2009), "Tax competition and harmonization in Southeast Asia", Massey University, Albany, New Zealand, *http://mro.massey.ac.nz/bitstream/handle/10179/966/02whole.pdf?sequence=1&isAllowed=y*.

Bessho, S. (2016), "Case Study of Central and Local Government Finance in Japan", *ADBI Working Paper* No 599, Asian Development Bank Institute, Tokyo, *https://www.adb.org /publications/case-study-central-and-local-government-finance-japan/*.

BOC (2015), "BOC 2015 annual report", Bureau of Customs, Manilla, *http://customs.gov.ph/*.

Brondolo J. et al. (2008), *Tax Administration Reform and Fiscal Adjustment: The Case of Indonesia (2001-07)*, International Monetary Fund, Washington, DC, *https://www.imf.org/external/pubs/ft/wp/2008/wp08129.pdf*.

DOF (2017), "Gov't losing P91 B yearly from VAT exemptions", *www.dof.gov.ph/taxreform/index.php/2017/05/18/govt-losing-p91-b-yearly-from-vat-exemptions/*.

DOF (2016), "PHL's low tax efficiency requires reforms", *www.dof.gov.ph/index.php/phls-low-tax-efficiency-requires-reforms/*.

EPS PEAKS (2013), "Taxation and Developing Countries", Overseas Development Institute training notes, London, *https://www.odi.org/sites/odi.org.uk/files/odi-assets/events-documents/5045.pdf*.

Ernst and Young (2015), *Indirect taxes in 2015*, EYG no. DL1195, *www.ey.com/Publication/vwLUAssets/ ey-indirect-tax-developments-in-2015/%24FILE/ey-indirect-tax-developments-in-2015.pdf*.

Gupta, P. (2015), "Generating Larger Tax Revenue in South Asia", *MPRA Paper*, No. 61443, *https://mpra. ub.uni-muenchen.de/61443/1/MPRA_paper_61443.pdf*.

IBFD (2017), International Bureau of Fiscal Documentation (website), *https://www.ibfd.org/*.

IMF (2017), "Indonesia, selected issues", *IMF Country Report* No. 17/48, International Monetary Fund, Washington, DC, *https://www.imf.org/~/media/Files/Publications/CR/2017/cr1748.ashx*.

IMF (2016), *World Economic Outlook – Frequently Asked Questions*, *https://www.imf.org/external/pubs/ft/weo /faq.htm#q4d*.

IMF (2015), *World Economic Outlook: Adjusting to Lower Commodity Prices*, International Monetary Fund, Washington, DC, October.

Indonesia investments (2017), "Tax system of Indonesia", *https://www.indonesia-investments.com/finance/ tax-system/item277?*.

Inland Revenue Board of Malaysia (2016), "Agriculture allowances public ruling no. 1/2016", *www.hasil. gov.my/pdf/pdfam/PR_01_2016.pdf*.

IPSS (2014), "Social Security in Japan 2014", National Institute of Population and Social Security Research, Tokyo, *www.ipss.go.jp/s-info/e/ssj2014/pdf/SSJ2014.pdf*.

KPMG (2016), "Corporate tax rates table", *https://home.kpmg.com/xx/en/home/services/tax/tax-tools- and-resources/tax-rates-online/corporate-tax-rates-table.html*.

Ministry of International Trade and Industry (2016), Kuala Lumpur, Malaysia, *www.miti.gov.my/index. php/pages/view/content5235.html*.

MOF (2017), *www.mof.gov.sg/Policies/Tax-Policies/Goods-and-Services-Tax*.

Newhouse D. and D. Zakharova (2007) *Distributional Implications of the VAT Reform in the Philippines*, International Monetary Fund, Washington, DC, *https://www.imf.org/external/pubs/ft/wp/2007/ wp07153.pdf*.

Nugraha, K. and P. Lewis (2011), "Market Income, Actual Income and Income Distribution in Indonesia", 40th Australian Conference of Economists paper, Canberra, *http://ace2011.org.au/ACE2011/Documents/ Abstract_Kunta_Nugraha_Phil_Lewis.pdf*.

OECD (2016a), *Revenue Statistics 2016*, OECD Publishing, Paris, *http://dx.doi.org/10.1787/rev_stats-2016-en-fr*.

OECD (2016b), *Economic Outlook for Southeast Asia, China and India 2016: Enhancing Regional Ties*, OECD Publishing, Paris, *http://dx.doi.org/10.1787/saeo-2016-en*.

OECD (2016c), *Consumption Tax Trends 2016: VAT/GST and Excise Rates, Trends and Policy Issues*, OECD Publishing, Paris, *http://dx.doi.org/10.1787/ctt-2016-en*.

OECD, et al. (2016), *Revenue Statistics in Latin America and the Caribbean 2016*, OECD Publishing, Paris, *http:// dx.doi.org/10.1787/rev_lat_car-2016-en-fr*.

OECD (2015a), *OECD Economic Surveys: Indonesia*, OECD Publishing, Paris, *http://dx.doi.org/10.1787/ eco_surveys-idn-2015-en*.

OECD (2015b), *Revenue Statistics in Asian Countries 2015: Trends in Indonesia, Malaysia and the Philippines*, OECD Publishing, Paris, *http://dx.doi.org/10.1787/9789264234277-en*.

OECD (2014), *Development Co-operation Report 2014: Mobilising Resources for Sustainable Development*, OECD Publishing, Paris, *http://dx.doi.org/10.1787/dcr-2014-en*.

Oxford Business Group (2014), *The Report: Malaysia 2014*, Oxford Business Group, *www.oxfordbusinessgroup. com/malaysia-2014*.

Papageorgiou, C. et al. (2015), "Diversification, Growth, and Volatility in Asia", *World Bank Policy Research Working Paper*, No 7380, *http://documents.worldbank.org/curated/en/271261467986248043/pdf/ WPS7380.pdf*.

PKF (2015) "Indonesia Tax Guide 2015/16", PKF international limited, *www.pkf.com/media/10026000/ indonesia-tax-guide-2015-16.pdf*.

Pomfret, R. and P. Sourdin (2011), "Trade Agreements in Southeast Asia", *https://www.wto.org/english/ res_e/publications_e/wtr11_forum_e/wtr11_2feb11_e.htm*.

Profeta, P. and S. Scabrosetti (2010), *The Political Economy of Taxation: Lessons from Developing Countries*, Edward Elgar Publishing, *https://books.google.fr/books?isbn=1849805490*.

Safuan, S. (2012), "ASEAN Economic Cooperation: Trade Liberalization Impacts on the National Economy", *International Journal of Economics and Finance*, Vol. 4, No. 11, Canadian Center of Science and Education, *http://dx.doi.org/10.5539/ijef.v4n11p66*.

SSA (2000), "Public Pension Reform in Japan", *Social Security Bulletin*, Vol. 63, No. 4, *https://www.ssa.gov/policy/docs/ssb/v63n4/v63n4p99.pdf*.

The Philippine Star (2016), "Despite strong GDP growth Tax collection slows in Q1", *www.philstar.com/business/2016/05/21/1585219/despite-strong-gdp-growth-tax-collection-slows-q1*.

Tradingeconomics (2016), *www.tradingeconomics.com/search.aspx?q=VATrate*.

UNCTAD (2012), *World Investment Report 2012, Towards a new Generation of Investment Policies*, New York and Geneva, *http://unctad.org/en/PublicationsLibrary/wir2012_embargoed_en.pdf*.

UNESCAP (2016), "Improving tax policy and administration in South-East Asia", *MPFD policy briefs* No. 31, *https://www.unescap.org/sites/default/files/MPFD%20Policy%20Briefs%20No.31-SEA.pdf*.

UNESCAP (2014), *Economic and Social Survey of Asia and the Pacific 2014, Regional Connectivity for Shared Prosperity*, United Nations, *https://www.unescap.org/sites/default/files/Economic%20and%20Social%20Survey%20of%20Asia%20and%20the%20Pacific%202014.pdf*.

WHO (2015), "Purchasing Power Parity 2005", *www.who.int/choice/costs/ppp/en/*.

Chapter 2

SPECIAL FEATURE
Electronic services in tax administration

The level of tax revenues in an economy is influenced by tax policy and tax administration as well as the level of taxpayer compliance and government enforcement. Developments in information and communication technology (ICT) in recent decades, both for electronic filing and payment of taxes, have presented many opportunities for revenue bodies to increase government revenue, improve efficiency, and enhance the quality of services delivered to taxpayers, while at the same time reducing taxpayer compliance burden and government administration costs, and improving enforcement.

While the attention of revenue bodies was initially focused on the computerisation of routine tax administration processes (e.g. taxpayer registration and revenue accounting), the later part of the last decade and the early part of this decade saw most tax administrations tailoring their websites to provide transaction services as well as online forms and calculators for taxpayers. Initially many of the services concentrate on the electronic filing of tax returns for the major taxes and the electronic payment of taxes. Subsequently administrations adopted more two-way services including alerts and notifications. They also developed automated systems and processes for exchanging taxpayer data between businesses, government bodies and revenue bodies.

More recently administrations have developed:

- Systems that, subject to security safeguards, provide taxpayers with online access to their own taxpayer information (e.g. registration and accounting details);
- Mobile applications that allow taxpayers to undertake inquiries on their tax account and increasingly to be able to pay and file;
- Self-service options, especially utilising technologies that allow the provision of more personalised services and automated support.

2.1. Successfully harnessing ICT opportunities presents numerous challenges for revenue bodies

The leveraging of ICT for the modernisation of public administration and service delivery is receiving increased attention from governments and donor agencies. ICT enables governments to minimise the time, cost and resources to deliver taxpayer services, which has led to enhanced convenience, transparency and trust in the public service. Taxpayers no longer need to go to the tax office personally and wait to file their tax returns, or send mail. At the same time, some public sector ICT projects have received criticism for not delivering the desired results and for leading to unproductive investments without much improvement in the quality of service delivery.

Many factors have influenced the outcomes of ICT projects, including:

- Proper planning and prioritisation for ICT investments;
- Standardisation of work processes for project implementation;
- Instituting strong governance structures; and
- Applying staged implementation phases based on the likelihood of potential benefits.

The vast majority of economies in the Asian region reported having a formal plan or strategy for improving the range and quality of their electronic taxpayer services over the medium term (Table 2.1). The priority areas most frequently reported were the online filing of tax returns, online payment of taxes, enhanced websites that include more information and facilities (e.g. tax calculator), other online transactions, and integrated taxpayer accounts.

Table 2.1. **Strategic priorities for increased use of online services**

Economy	Type of electronic service							
	Online filing	Pre-filled returns	Online payment	Website service or tools	Integrated taxpayer accounts	Other online services	Enhanced data capture	Digital mailbox[1]
Brunei Darussalam	✓		✓	✓				✓
Cambodia	✓			✓		✓		
Hong Kong, China	✓	✓		✓		✓		
Indonesia	✓	✓	✓			✓	✓	
Japan	✓		✓	✓				
Korea	✓		✓		✓	✓		✓
Kyrgyzstan	✓		✓	✓	✓		✓	✓
Lao PDR								
Malaysia	✓	✓	✓	✓		✓		
Maldives	✓		✓	✓	✓	✓		
Mongolia	✓	✓	✓	✓				✓
Papua New Guinea	✓	✓	✓		✓		✓	
Philippines	✓		✓	✓	✓	✓	✓	✓
Singapore	✓	✓				✓	✓	✓
Tajikistan	✓							
Thailand	✓		✓	✓	✓		✓	

Notes: Lao PDR = Lao People's Democratic Republic. The absence of a tick mark means the type of service was not reported as a priority.
1. The digital mailbox is an e-mail support enabling taxpayers to seek clarification or guidance on Tax MIS application and services.
Sources: ADB (2016) and OECD (2015) survey responses.

StatLink ⬛⬛ http://dx.doi.org/10.1787/888933543847

2.2. Use of electronic filing for key tax types

Electronic tax return filing systems are one of the most visible ITC-based services available to taxpayers. For many personal taxpayers, the submission of annual income tax returns is their most significant contact with the revenue agency, and a system enabling taxpayers to submit their tax returns electronically can be of benefit to both taxpayers and the government: taxpayers benefit from a simpler and more convenient system, reducing compliance effort and uncertainty and (in some cases) streamlining payment of taxes; while governments benefit from a reduced administrative burden that can be gained through the direct provision of taxpayer information in standardised electronic form, and increased compliance. Similarly, businesses can also benefit from electronic filing systems, in particular those that simplify compliance with the corporate income tax (CIT) and value-added tax (VAT) regimes and with those that facilitate withholding of employees' personal income taxes (PIT).

There are significant benefits from implementing well-designed and widely used systems of electronic filing:

● Reductions in taxpayers' compliance burden: Returns can be completed online, and taxpayers do not have to waste time obtaining paper returns and instructions. Similarly, refunds of overpaid taxes can be delivered more quickly than when paper documentation systems are used.

- Improved data quality: Many data items can be validated as they are input by taxpayers, meaning that the quality of data transmitted is of a higher standard.

- Reductions in revenue bodies' operational costs: Considerably fewer staff are required to process electronically filed returns.

- Improved overall management of the tax system: Taxpayer records can be updated more quickly, and management information can be more readily compiled and shared.

One of the significant innovations in tax return process design over the last two decades has been the development of pre-filled tax returns, primarily for personal income taxpayers. The pre-filled approach involves administrations "pre-populating" the taxpayer's return or online account with information it has collected from third parties. The pre-filled return can be reviewed by the taxpayer and either filed "on line" or in paper form. As the extent of pre-population is generally determined by the range of electronic data sources available to the administration, it is critical to this approach that the legislative framework provides extensive and timely third-party reporting covering all relevant taxpayer information.

Experience from many economies suggests that implementing systems of electronic filing can present many challenges for revenue bodies, particularly those with limited ICT experience. For example, there are times when agency staff are slow to adopt new technologies. Even after many years, the system's facilities may remain unused. This can be due to a lack of management buy-in before implementation, lack of involvement of staff in early trial runs, and a multi-layered decision-making structure leading to a lack of clear vision on the goals of the ICT programme. Such a failure creates doubts about ICT systems in the minds of staff and has a cascading effect on the implementation of future ICT programmes.

In addition, it can take several years to achieve substantial progress in their use by taxpayers. Generally speaking, revenue bodies in advanced economies in Asia (e.g. Japan, Korea and Singapore) have a relatively high percentage of tax returns filed electronically while developing countries continue to increase the percentage of electronic returns (Table 2.2). Increased use of online filing of tax returns is being achieved by a number of emerging and developing economies (e.g. Malaysia, Mongolia and Thailand). However, for many developing economies (e.g. Cambodia; Hong Kong, China; Kyrgyzstan; Papua New Guinea; the Philippines; and Tajikistan), either very limited progress has been made in this regard, or such services are yet to be offered.

Revenue bodies in most advanced economies have made substantial progress with the implementation of electronic filing for personal income taxes and corporate income taxes, although for many this has been achieved only after many years of promotion and refinement of the service offered. Revenue bodies in several developing economies have made rapid advances with electronic filing in recent years. For example, 83% of tax returns were filed electronically in Malaysia in 2013, up from 69% in 2011. Thailand's usage of electronic tax filing has increased from 10% to 75% for corporate income taxes between 2011 and 2013. Many revenue bodies have achieved success with electronic filing by mandating its use for larger businesses.

Use of electronic tax filing is still quite rare in most developing countries (e.g. Cambodia, Kyrgyzstan, the Maldives, Papua New Guinea, the Philippines and Tajikistan) and there is significant potential for them to make substantial progress. In the Maldives, the use of e-filing began in December 2014. Its strategic priorities for the period 2015-19 include enabling online payment and filing for all taxes, and ensuring that at least 75% of tax returns are filed online and that 50% of payments are made online. Papua New Guinea began the use of electronic filing in 2014.

Table 2.2. **Rates of electronic tax filing for the major taxes, 2011 and 2013**

Economy	Percentage of total number of returns filed electronically					
	Personal income tax		Corporate income tax		Value-added tax	
	2011	2013	2011	2013	2011	2013
Brunei Darussalam	No PIT in place		..	51	No VAT in place	
Cambodia	0	0	0	0	0	0
Hong Kong, China	14	15	<1	<1	No VAT in place	
Indonesia	..	<1	..	5	..	57
Japan	44	50	58	64	53	63
Korea	87	91	97	98	79	83
Kyrgyzstan	<1	<1	3	8	37	1.5
Malaysia	69	83	49	76	No VAT in place	
Maldives	No PIT in place		0	0	0	0
Mongolia	..	..	76	80	96	92
Papua New Guinea	0	0	0	0	0	0
Philippines	<1	1	9	14	12	16
Singapore	96	97	63	69	100	100
Tajikistan	0	0	0	0	0	0
Thailand	45	34	10	75	14	69

Notes: PIT = personal income tax, VAT = value-added tax. ".." = data not available. Malaysia implemented a VAT in 2015.

Source: ADB (2016) and OECD (2015) survey responses.

StatLink http://dx.doi.org/10.1787/888933543866

2.3. Using electronic payment methods for collecting taxes

The payment of taxes is another important interaction between taxpayers (particularly businesses) and revenue bodies, and one where the use of ICT can deliver significant benefits to taxpayers, revenue bodies, government, and the financial sector. For taxpayers, there can be significant costs in visiting a revenue office (or its agent such as a bank) during business hours to make a tax payment. Even paying by mailed cheques presents a fair compliance cost to the taxpayer. For payments made in either of these ways, there is also the cost of manually processing these payments, and there can be a time delay before a taxpayer's account is updated. On the other hand, payment methods that are fully electronic have been shown to be significantly less costly to administer, and typically enable quicker updating of taxpayers' accounts.

Historically, virtually all revenue bodies provided in-person payment services or promoted the use of mailed payments by cheque, referred to as non-electronic payment methods, due in part to the absence of alternatives (Table 2.3). However, over time with increased digitalisation, it became more cost effective for revenue bodies to use third parties such as banks to collect tax payments, with relevant payment data being transmitted by banks to the government electronically to enable them to update taxpayers' records. This is referred to as a partially electronic payment method. A more recent development is the fully electronic payment method, in which taxpayers make their own payments online (or arrange for this to be done automatically via their bank with a direct-debit type of arrangement). Studies undertaken thus far clearly indicate that fully electronic payment methods are by far the most cost-effective means of collecting tax payments (OECD, 2010).

Table 2.3. **Tax payment methods available and volume usage, 2013**

Economy	Type of payment method and percentage share in total number of payments (where known)						
	Non-electronic		Partially electronic		Fully electronic		
	Mailed check	In-person at office	Agency payment	Phone banking	Internet	Direct debit	Payment kiosk
Brunei Darussalam	✓	✓	✓		✓	✓	
Cambodia		✓	✓				
China, People's Rep. of	✓	✓	✓	✓	✓	✓	
Hong Kong, China	✓ (6)		✓ (38)	✓ (17)	✓ (31)		✓ (8)
Indonesia			✓		✓		
Japan			✓ (75)		✓ (2)	✓ (15)	
Korea		✓ (5)	✓ (60)	✓ (<1)	✓ (25)	✓ (4)	✓ (6)
Kyrgyzstan		✓	✓			✓	✓
Malaysia	✓	✓ (51)	✓ (43)	✓	✓ (6)	✓	✓
Maldives		✓ (100)					
Mongolia			✓	✓	✓	✓	
Papua New Guinea	✓ (20)	✓ (70)			✓ (5)	✓ (5)	
Philippines		✓ (<1)	✓ (93)		✓ (7)		
Singapore	✓ (12)	✓ (7)		(10)	✓ (50)	✓ (17)	✓ (5)
Tajikistan	..	..	..	..	..	..	..
Thailand		✓ (70)	✓ (<1)		✓ (29)		

Notes: ".." = data not available. The absence of a tick mark means method is not available. Information for Mongolia refers to 2014 except for the partially electronic agency payment.

Sources: ADB (2016) and OECD (2015) survey responses.

StatLink ᵐˢᵖ *http://dx.doi.org/10.1787/888933543885*

While many economies report the use of a comprehensive suite of electronic and non-electronic payment methods, many do not have statistics on the use of these tools, limiting their understanding and knowledge of taxpayer practices and the costs and value of their respective methods. A list of useful statistics may include:

- Total number of registration applications received on line (% of total registered taxpayers);
- Number of filings made on line (% of total transactions);
- Number of tax payments made at banks (% of total transactions);
- Number of tax payments made on line (% of total transactions);
- Total number of appeals submitted on line (% of total appeals); and
- Total number of tax filings made on line by large taxpayer units (% of total large taxpayers), etc.

Around half of revenue bodies surveyed reported the use of in-person at-office payment methods in 2013 which, as already indicated, are generally the costliest payment methods used for collecting taxes. For a few economies, the reported volumes of such payments were relatively high at 51% (Malaysia), 100% (Maldives), 70% (Papua New Guinea), and 70% (Thailand). Very high rate of use of fully electronic methods was reported by Singapore at 50% in 2013.

The Maldives and Mongolia both reported that new online payment services were implemented in 2014 or 2015, while Papua New Guinea reported that more taxpayers made direct debit payments in 2014 and 2015 than previously.

2.4. Progress of electronic tax services in Southeast Asian countries and Kazakhstan

Since 2000, Southeast Asian countries have undertaken a number of steps to improve the provision and capability of ICT services for tax filing and payments. Several developments are reported in this section.

Indonesia started to advocate a more intensive use of information technology in 2002 as part of its efforts to reform the Directorate General of Taxation (DGT) with support from international donors such as the World Bank. This reform has led to an updating of administrative processes, including the introduction of electronic filing and registration, and risk analysis. The amount of time required to pay taxes has been cut by more than half, from 560 hours in 2006 to 266 hours in 2011 since DGT introduced electronic tax services (World Bank, 2012).

A more recent project related to promoting electronic tax services was started in 2011 as the DGT developed Modul Penerimaan Negara Generasi 2 (MPN-G2, or Second Generation State Revenue Module) to improve the efficiency of state revenue administration. MPN-G2 included a number of new features, such as allowing payment of all taxes, accommodating payments in US dollars, and allowing tax payments to be made via automated teller machine or internet banking with a unique e-Billing ID generated online (KPMG, 2016). After years of piloting in selected banks and regions in Indonesia, DGT formally introduced MPN-G2 nationwide in January 2016 and made its use mandatory for all tax payments after June 2016. The web-based MPN-G2 is simple to use and can be accessed on any device that has internet connection, including tablets and smart phones, without installing additional software. However, there are a number of challenges that remain to be addressed, including a compatibility issue with some devices, technical problems such as bugs when using the website and poor ICT infrastructure and internet connections in Indonesia, especially outside of Java, which could cause frustrations for taxpayers (KPMG, 2016).

In **Malaysia**, the Inland Revenue Board (IRB) of Malaysia started an initiative to implement an electronic system for filing and paying taxes to promote paperless transactions in 2004 (World Bank, 2013). The new system allows taxpayers to complete tax forms and provide required payment details on line. This comprehensive system now consists of ByrHASiL, which allows online payment of income tax through appointed banks; e-Daftar, which allows online income tax file registration by new taxpayers; e-Filing, which allows electronic filling and submission of income tax return forms; e-Kemaskini, which facilitates information updates by taxpayers; and other online services that offer assistance to corporate taxpayers.

During the implementation of this new electronic system, Malaysia faced many challenges. For example, many taxpayers were reluctant to abandon the traditional paper-based process due to uncertainty about the security and privacy of information. The server was slow and often failed so taxpayers willing to try the new technology were discouraged. In order to address these problems, IRB applied several upgrades to the system and spent significant efforts advertising and promoting the safety and ease of its usage. Incentives have been offered for taxpayers using the electronic system, such as deadline extensions for tax filing, lower penalties for late submissions of tax returns, and more speedy refunds of excess taxes. As a result, the share of individuals and companies filing electronically has increased from 5% in 2006 to 34% in 2011 while tax compliance time has reduced from 190 hours in 2004 to 133 hours in 2010 (World Bank, 2013).

The Bureau of Internal Revenue (BIR) of the **Philippines** developed and introduced the Electronic Filing and Payment System (eFPS) in 2001, to simplify the tax processing in accordance with the Electronic Commerce Act passed in 2000. The electronic system aims to provide high quality and convenient service by achieving faster processing and immediate confirmation of the filing of tax returns. Unlike the traditional paper-based system where taxpayers have to manually file tax returns to various revenue district offices scattered across the country, eFPS allows users to directly fill in and submit their taxes on line through the BIR website. The system also helps BIR to gather tax related data in a faster and more reliable way.

However, despite the growing popularity of the internet, few taxpayers are using the electronic filing and payment system. BIR noted that only 3% of taxpayers submitted their payments on line in 2014. This is partly due to lack of awareness about the service and partly due to problems with the system itself. The biggest problem with eFPS is its unreliability as a result of numerous technical problems and limited system availability since its launch. Some of these technical problems could be very costly. For example, the malfunction of eFPS caused a domestic company, Maersk Filipinas, to submit its withholding taxes payment three times in 2002. The subsequent lawsuit to reclaim the overpaid taxes took five years (Rafal, 2012). In order to increase use of the system, BIR has passed regulations that mandate the use of the electronic tax system for certain taxpayers in 2015 while penalties will be imposed for non-compliance.

Singapore was one of the first countries in Asia to adopt an electronic system in public administration. Electronic tax services in Singapore are relatively well developed compared to other countries in the region. The share of small companies using e-Filing has grown steadily from 22% in 2012 to 41% in 2014 (IRAS, 2015).

The Inland Revenue Authority of Singapore (IRAS) was created in 1992 to administer taxes and start developing an integrated and computerised system for tax administration. IRAS first introduced an imaging system to electronically process the paper-based returns filed by citizens which lowered the time needed to issue tax assessments from 12-18 months to 3-5 months (World Bank, 2000). Direct electronic filing through internet was introduced in 1998. While only small companies could file their tax returns electronically in the past, IRAS announced the extension of E-filing to all companies regardless of firm size in 2015.

In addition to submitting returns electronically, taxpayers can also pay taxes electronically. A 12-month interest-free instalment plan (based on the previous year's tax assessment) is offered, under which tax is deducted directly from bank accounts. Changes in tax liabilities automatically lead to adjustments in payments. Alternatively, taxpayers can pay a lump sum once their current liability is assessed through direct deduction, by phone or internet banking services, or by debit card at payment kiosks or taxpayer service centres.

In **Kazakhstan,** the State Revenue Committee (SRC) is a department of the Ministry of Finance, which carries out regulatory, trade and control functions for the completeness and accuracy of tax receipts, customs and other payments into the budget, tax computations, etc. The SRC provides individuals and legal entities with 48 state services, including 29 tax services and 19 customs services. In order to improve services provided to beneficiaries, SRC continuously works on translating public services into electronic format. To date, 32 out of 48 public services (or 66.6%) have been automated, including 28 through the e-government portal. One of the most popular electronic services provided by SRC is the receipt of tax reports. The share of tax reporting submitted electronically for 2016 was 95%. According to a new policy, all VAT payers were supposed to switch to electronic VAT invoices on 1 January 2017. The implementation has been postponed to 2018 for 300 largest taxpayers and to 2019 for all other VAT payers as the government aims for a smoother transition.

References

ADB (2016), *A Comparative Analysis of Tax Administration in Asia and the Pacific*, ADB Tax Administration Survey, Asian Development Bank, Manila, *https://www.adb.org/sites/default/files/publication/193541/tax-admin-asia-pacific-2016.pdf*.

IRAS (2015), "Corporate Tax Season 2015: IRAS Extends Convenience of e-Filing to All Companies", Inland Revenue Authority of Singapore, *https://www.iras.gov.sg/irashome/News-and-Events/Newsroom/Media-Releases-and-Speeches/Media-Releases/2015/Corporate-Tax-Season-2015--IRAS-Extends-Convenience-of-e-Filing-to-All-Companies/*.

KPMG (2016), "Tax News Flash: New Electronic Tax Payment System Requirements", *https://assets.kpmg.com/content/dam/kpmg/pdf/2016/06/id-kai-tax-news-flash-january-2016-electronic-tax-payment.pdf*.

OECD (2015), *Tax Administration 2015: Comparative Information on OECD and Other Advanced and Emerging Economies*, OECD Publishing, Paris, *http://dx.doi.org/10.1787/tax_admin-2015-en*.

OECD (2010), *Survey of Trends and Developments in the Use of Electronic Services for Taxpayer Service Delivery*, OECD Forum on Tax Administration, Paris, *www.oecd.org/tax/administration/45035933.pdf*.

Rafal, C.L. (2012), "A Look at the BIR'S EFPS", AUSL Tech & Law, 26 September, *https://ausltechlaw.wordpress.com/2012/09/26/rafal-cherry-liez-a-look-at-the-birs-efps/*.

World Bank (2013), *Doing Business 2014: Understanding Regulations for Small and Medium-Sized Enterprises*, World Bank, Washington, DC.

World Bank (2012), *Doing Business in Indonesia*, World Bank, Washington, DC.

World Bank (2000), *Improving Taxpayer Service and Facilitating Compliance in Singapore*, World Bank, Washington, DC.

Chapter 3

Tax levels and tax structures, 1990-2015

3.1. Comparative tables, 1990-2015

In all of the following tables (..) indicates not available. The main series in this volume cover the years 1990 to 2015.

Figures referring to 1991-96 in Table 3.1 and figures relating to 1990-96, 1998-99, 2001-04 and 2006-08 in Tables 3.4 to 3.19 have been omitted because of lack of space. Complete series are available on line at *http://stats.oecd.org/*.

Table 3.1. **Total tax revenue as percentage of GDP, 1990-2015**

	1990	1997	1998	1999	2000	2001	2002	2003	2004	2005
Indonesia[1]	..	9.1	7.4	9.3	8.6	11.9	12.3	12.9	13.2	13.5
Kazakhstan	..	..	12.3	15.9	19.8	22.2	20.5	22.7	21.7	25.5
Malaysia[2]	19.1	20.2	17.2	16.3	14.6	18.9	18.9	17.0	16.6	16.1
Philippines	..	16.7	15.5	15.8	15.8	15.6	15.0	15.0	14.6	15.2
Singapore	..	..	..	..	15.5	15.1	13.1	12.7	12.3	12.1
OECD Average[3]	32.0	33.6	33.7	33.9	34.0	33.5	33.2	33.2	33.1	33.6
Japan[3]	28.5	26.8	26.4	25.9	26.6	26.8	25.8	25.3	26.1	27.3
Korea[3]	18.8	19.4	19.4	19.7	21.5	21.8	21.9	22.7	22.0	22.5

	2006	2007	2008	2009	2010	2011	2012	2013	2014	2015
Indonesia[1]	13.0	13.3	14.2	11.9	11.4	12.2	12.5	12.5	12.2	11.8
Kazakhstan	26.1	26.1	27.6	21.2	23.8	24.5	23.9	22.6	21.1	15.5
Malaysia[2]	15.7	15.4	15.7	16.1	14.4	15.8	16.6	16.3	15.9	15.3
Philippines	16.5	16.3	16.2	15.0	14.8	15.1	15.8	16.2	16.7	17.0
Singapore	12.3	13.5	13.9	13.1	13.0	13.3	13.9	13.5	13.9	13.6
OECD Average[3]	33.7	33.8	33.2	32.4	32.6	33.0	33.4	33.8	34.2	34.3
Japan[3]	28.1	28.5	28.5	27.0	27.6	28.6	29.4	30.3	32.0	..
Korea[3]	23.6	24.8	24.6	23.8	23.4	24.2	24.8	24.3	24.6	25.3

.. Not available

1. The figures exclude social security contributions. The figures for social security contributions (heading 2000) are not available but they are thought to be negligible as they relate only to the "Asuransi Kesehatan" - a health insurance programme for employees in for-profit state-owned enterprises.

2. The data are estimated for 2015 (social security contributions and property taxes).

3. The OECD average represents the unweighted average for OECD member countries. Japan and Korea are also part of the OECD (35) group. Data for Japan, Korea and the OECD average are taken from OECD (2016), Revenue Statistics 2016, *http://dx.doi.org/10.1787/rev_stats-2016-en-fr*.

StatLink *http://dx.doi.org/10.1787/888933543904*

Table 3.2. **Tax revenue of main headings as percentage of GDP, 2015**

	1000 Income & profits	2000 Social security	3000 Payroll	4000 Property	5000 Goods & services	6000 Other
Indonesia[1]	5.2	..	0.0	0.3	5.2	1.1
Kazakhstan	6.0	0.6	1.1	0.6	7.2	0.0
Malaysia[2]	9.1	0.3	0.0	0.5	4.9	0.5
Philippines	6.9	2.4	0.0	0.5	6.6	0.6
Singapore[3]	6.1	0.0	0.0	1.8	4.3	1.4
OECD Average[4,5]	11.6	9.1	0.4	1.9	11.0	0.2
Japan[6]	10.4	12.7	0.0	2.6	6.8	0.1
Korea[5]	7.6	6.7	0.1	3.1	7.1	0.6

.. Not available

1. The figures exclude social security contributions. The figures for social security contributions (heading 2000) are not available but they are thought to be negligible as they relate only to the "Asuransi Kesehatan" - a health insurance programme for employees in for-profit state-owned enterprises.

2. The data are estimated for 2015 (social security contributions and property taxes).

3. There are no social security contributions in Singapore.

4. Represents the unweighted average for OECD member countries. Japan and Korea are also part of the OECD (35) group. Data for 2014 are used for headings 2000, 3000, 4000, 5000 and 6000.

5. Data for Japan, Korea and the OECD average are taken from OECD (2016), Revenue Statistics 2016, *http://dx.doi.org/10.1787/rev_stats-2016-en-fr*, and are preliminary for 2015.

6. Data for 2014 are used for heading 2000 (social security contributions).

StatLink *http://dx.doi.org/10.1787/888933543923*

Table 3.3. **Tax revenue of main headings as percentage of total taxation, 2015**

	1000 Income & profits	2000 Social security	3000 Payroll	4000 Property	5000 Goods & services	6000 Other
Indonesia[1]	44.2	..	0.0	2.1	44.3	9.3
Kazakhstan	38.8	3.8	7.3	3.6	46.5	0.0
Malaysia[2]	59.6	1.6	0.0	3.6	31.8	3.4
Philippines	40.3	14.0	0.0	2.8	39.1	3.8
Singapore[3]	44.7	0.0	0.0	13.0	31.7	10.6
OECD Average[4,5,6]	33.7	26.2	1.1	5.6	32.6	0.7
Japan[5,6]	31.8	39.7	0.0	8.5	19.8	0.3
Korea[6]	30.3	26.6	0.3	12.4	28.0	2.4

.. Not available

1. The figures exclude social security contributions. The figures for social security contributions (heading 2000) are not available but they are thought to be negligible as they relate only to the "Asuransi Kesehatan" - a health insurance programme for employees in for-profit state-owned enterprises.
2. The data are estimated for 2015 (social security contributions and property taxes).
3. There are no social security contributions in Singapore.
4. Represents the unweighted average for OECD member countries. Japan and Korea are also part of the OECD (35) group.
5. Data for 2014 are used for all the headings.
6. Data for Japan, Korea and the OECD average are taken from OECD (2016), Revenue Statistics 2016, http://dx.doi.org/10.1787/rev_stats-2016-en-fr.

StatLink http://dx.doi.org/10.1787/888933543942

Table 3.4. **Taxes on income and profits (1000) as percentage of GDP**

	1997	2000	2005	2009	2010	2011	2012	2013	2014	2015
Indonesia	4.3	4.1	6.3	5.7	5.2	5.5	5.4	5.3	5.2	5.2
Kazakhstan	..	8.3	13.2	10.1	9.5	9.4	9.1	8.1	7.8	6.0
Malaysia	9.8	7.7	9.4	10.6	9.1	10.8	11.5	11.2	10.9	9.1
Philippines	6.1	6.1	6.1	5.8	5.8	6.3	6.5	6.7	6.6	6.9
Singapore	..	8.2	6.1	6.2	5.8	5.9	6.2	5.8	6.1	6.1
OECD Average[1]	11.6	12.0	11.7	10.9	10.8	11.0	11.2	11.4	11.5	11.6
Japan[1]	9.9	9.3	9.2	8.0	8.3	8.6	9.1	9.9	10.2	10.4
Korea[1]	5.1	6.2	6.6	6.8	6.6	7.3	7.4	7.1	7.2	7.6

.. Not available

1. The OECD average represents the unweighted average for OECD member countries. Japan and Korea are also part of the OECD (35) group. Data for Japan, Korea and the OECD average are taken from OECD (2016), Revenue Statistics 2016, http://dx.doi.org/10.1787/rev_stats-2016-en-fr, and are preliminary for 2015.

StatLink http://dx.doi.org/10.1787/888933543961

Table 3.5. **Taxes on income and profits (1000) as percentage of total taxation**

	1997	2000	2005	2009	2010	2011	2012	2013	2014	2015
Indonesia	47.2	47.7	46.8	47.8	45.8	45.2	43.2	42.5	42.5	44.2
Kazakhstan	..	41.7	51.7	47.9	40.0	38.5	38.2	36.0	37.2	38.8
Malaysia	48.6	52.7	58.3	65.6	63.4	67.9	69.1	68.6	68.6	59.6
Philippines	36.6	38.6	39.9	38.8	39.2	41.7	41.4	41.1	39.8	40.3
Singapore	..	52.8	50.3	47.0	44.7	44.7	44.7	43.1	44.2	44.7
OECD Average[1]	34.2	34.9	34.5	33.5	33.2	33.5	33.7	33.8	33.7	..
Japan[1]	37.0	34.8	33.8	29.5	30.2	30.2	31.1	32.5	31.8	..
Korea[1]	26.2	28.8	29.2	28.5	28.0	30.1	29.9	29.3	29.1	30.3

.. Not available

1. The OECD average represents the unweighted average for OECD member countries. Japan and Korea are also part of the OECD (35) group. Data for Japan, Korea and the OECD average are taken from OECD (2016), Revenue Statistics 2016, http://dx.doi.org/10.1787/rev_stats-2016-en-fr, and are preliminary for 2015.

StatLink http://dx.doi.org/10.1787/888933543980

Table 3.6. **Social security contributions (2000) as percentage of GDP**

	1997	2000	2005	2009	2010	2011	2012	2013	2014	2015
Indonesia[1]	..	..	..	..	..	..	..	..	..	..
Kazakhstan	..	0.0	0.2	0.5	0.6	0.5	0.6	0.6	0.6	0.6
Malaysia[2]	0.0	0.3	0.3	0.3	0.2	0.2	0.2	0.2	0.2	0.3
Philippines	1.4	2.1	1.9	1.9	1.9	1.9	2.0	2.1	2.2	2.4
Singapore[3]	..	0.0	0.0	0.0	0.0	0.0	0.0	0.0	0.0	0.0
OECD Average[4]	8.7	8.6	8.5	8.9	8.8	8.9	9.0	9.1	9.1	..
Japan[4]	9.2	9.4	10.1	11.0	11.3	11.9	12.2	12.4	12.7	..
Korea[4]	2.7	3.6	4.8	5.6	5.5	5.8	6.1	6.4	6.6	6.7

.. Not available

1. The figures for social security contributions (heading 2000) are not available but they are thought to be negligible as they relate only to the "Asuransi Kesehatan" - a health insurance programme for employees in for-profit state-owned enterprises.
2. The data are estimated for 2015.
3. There are no social security contributions in Singapore.
4. The OECD average represents the unweighted average for OECD member countries. Japan and Korea are also part of the OECD (35) group. Data for Japan, Korea and the OECD average are taken from OECD (2016), Revenue Statistics 2016, *http://dx.doi.org/10.1787/rev_stats-2016-en-fr*, and are preliminary for 2015.

StatLink http://dx.doi.org/10.1787/888933543999

Table 3.7. **Social security contributions (2000) as percentage of total taxation**

	1997	2000	2005	2009	2010	2011	2012	2013	2014	2015
Indonesia[1]	..	..	..	..	..	..	..	..	..	..
Kazakhstan	..	0.0	0.7	2.5	2.5	2.2	2.5	2.5	2.7	3.8
Malaysia[2]	0.0	1.9	1.6	1.6	1.7	1.5	1.4	1.5	1.5	1.6
Philippines	8.1	13.1	12.5	12.9	12.7	12.7	12.9	12.7	13.5	14.0
Singapore[3]	..	0.0	0.0	0.0	0.0	0.0	0.0	0.0	0.0	0.0
OECD Average[4]	25.1	24.8	25.3	26.8	26.6	26.4	26.4	26.3	26.2	..
Japan[4]	34.2	35.2	36.9	41.0	41.1	41.5	41.6	40.8	39.7	..
Korea[4]	14.2	16.7	21.2	23.4	23.3	24.0	24.7	26.4	26.9	26.6

.. Not available

1. The figures for social security contributions (heading 2000) are not available but they are thought to be negligible as they relate only to the "Asuransi Kesehatan" - a health insurance programme for employees in for-profit state-owned enterprises.
2. The data are estimated for 2015.
3. There are no social security contributions in Singapore.
4. The OECD average represents the unweighted average for OECD member countries. Japan and Korea are also part of the OECD (35) group. Data for Japan, Korea and the OECD average are taken from OECD (2016), Revenue Statistics 2016, *http://dx.doi.org/10.1787/rev_stats-2016-en-fr*, and are preliminary for 2015.

StatLink http://dx.doi.org/10.1787/888933544018

Table 3.8. **Taxes on property (4000) as percentage of GDP**

	1997	2000	2005	2009	2010	2011	2012	2013	2014	2015
Indonesia	0.4	0.3	0.7	0.5	0.5	0.4	0.3	0.3	0.2	0.3
Kazakhstan	..	0.8	0.6	0.6	0.6	0.5	0.5	0.4	0.5	0.6
Malaysia[1]	0.5	0.5	0.6	0.6	0.6	0.5	0.5	0.5	0.5	0.5
Philippines	0.2	0.5	0.5	0.5	0.4	0.5	0.5	0.5	0.5	0.5
Singapore	..	1.7	1.4	1.6	1.9	2.0	2.2	2.1	1.8	1.8
OECD Average[2]	1.7	1.8	1.8	1.7	1.7	1.8	1.8	1.9	1.9	..
Japan[2]	3.0	2.8	2.6	2.7	2.7	2.8	2.7	2.7	2.7	2.6
Korea[2]	2.5	2.7	2.7	2.8	2.6	2.7	2.6	2.5	2.7	3.1

.. Not available

1. The data are estimated for 2015.
2. The OECD average represents the unweighted average for OECD member countries. Japan and Korea are also part of the OECD (35) group. Data for Japan, Korea and the OECD average are taken from OECD (2016), Revenue Statistics 2016, *http://dx.doi.org/10.1787/rev_stats-2016-en-fr*, and are preliminary for 2015.

StatLink http://dx.doi.org/10.1787/888933544037

Table 3.9. **Taxes on property (4000) as percentage of total taxation**

	1997	2000	2005	2009	2010	2011	2012	2013	2014	2015
Indonesia	4.2	3.7	5.2	4.6	4.7	3.1	2.7	2.1	1.8	2.1
Kazakhstan	..	4.1	2.4	3.0	2.4	1.9	2.0	2.0	2.3	3.6
Malaysia[1]	2.5	3.4	3.9	3.9	4.0	3.5	3.2	3.2	3.4	3.6
Philippines	0.9	3.1	3.4	3.1	2.9	3.0	3.1	3.0	2.8	2.8
Singapore	..	11.2	11.2	11.9	14.5	15.4	16.1	15.9	13.2	13.0
OECD Average[2]	5.3	5.5	5.5	5.5	5.5	5.5	5.5	5.6	5.6	..
Japan[2]	11.2	10.5	9.7	10.1	9.7	9.7	9.1	8.8	8.5	..
Korea[2]	12.7	12.4	11.9	11.6	11.3	11.4	10.6	10.3	11.0	12.4

.. Not available

1. The data are estimated for 2015.
2. The OECD average represents the unweighted average for OECD member countries. Japan and Korea are also part of the OECD (35) group. Data for Japan, Korea and the OECD average are taken from OECD (2016), Revenue Statistics 2016, *http://dx.doi.org/10.1787/rev_stats-2016-en-fr*, and are preliminary for 2015.

StatLink *http://dx.doi.org/10.1787/888933544056*

Table 3.10. **Taxes on goods and services (5000) as percentage of GDP**

	1997	2000	2005	2009	2010	2011	2012	2013	2014	2015
Indonesia	4.3	3.9	5.4	4.8	4.7	5.2	5.6	5.7	5.4	5.2
Kazakhstan	..	6.9	9.0	8.5	11.9	13.1	12.6	12.4	11.1	7.2
Malaysia	8.9	5.6	5.4	4.2	3.9	3.7	3.8	3.7	3.6	4.9
Philippines	8.4	6.6	6.1	6.2	6.1	5.9	6.1	6.4	6.7	6.6
Singapore	..	4.8	4.1	4.5	4.5	4.4	4.2	4.2	4.3	4.3
OECD Average[1]	10.9	10.9	10.8	10.3	10.6	10.6	10.8	10.8	11.0	..
Japan[1]	4.6	5.1	5.3	5.1	5.1	5.3	5.3	5.3	6.3	6.8
Korea[1]	8.3	8.2	7.7	7.6	7.9	7.5	7.7	7.5	7.4	7.1

.. Not available

1. The OECD average represents the unweighted average for OECD member countries. Japan and Korea are also part of the OECD (35) group. Data for Japan, Korea and the OECD average are taken from OECD (2016), Revenue Statistics 2016, *http://dx.doi.org/10.1787/rev_stats-2016-en-fr*, and are preliminary for 2015.

StatLink *http://dx.doi.org/10.1787/888933544075*

Table 3.11. **Taxes on goods and services (5000) as percentage of total taxation**

	1997	2000	2005	2009	2010	2011	2012	2013	2014	2015
Indonesia	47.6	44.7	39.9	40.4	41.8	42.9	44.8	45.4	44.4	44.3
Kazakhstan	..	34.9	35.1	40.2	50.2	53.4	52.8	54.8	52.7	46.5
Malaysia	44.0	38.4	33.4	25.9	27.3	23.6	22.7	22.8	22.8	31.8
Philippines	50.2	42.0	39.9	41.4	41.3	38.7	38.8	39.4	40.0	39.1
Singapore	..	31.1	34.0	34.5	34.4	32.8	30.5	30.8	31.3	31.7
OECD Average[1]	33.4	33.0	32.9	32.3	32.9	32.7	32.6	32.4	32.6	..
Japan[1]	17.2	19.3	19.4	19.1	18.7	18.4	18.0	17.6	19.8	..
Korea[1]	42.7	38.4	34.3	31.8	33.7	31.2	31.2	30.7	30.0	28.0

.. Not available

1. The OECD average represents the unweighted average for OECD member countries. Japan and Korea are also part of the OECD (35) group. Data for Japan, Korea and the OECD average are taken from OECD (2016), Revenue Statistics 2016, *http://dx.doi.org/10.1787/rev_stats-2016-en-fr*, and are preliminary for 2015.

StatLink *http://dx.doi.org/10.1787/888933544094*

Table 3.12. **Taxes on general consumption (5110) as percentage of GDP**

	1997	2000	2005	2009	2010	2011	2012	2013	2014	2015
Indonesia	3.2	2.5	3.7	3.4	3.4	3.5	3.9	4.0	3.9	3.7
Kazakhstan	..	4.4	4.5	3.0	3.1	2.9	2.9	3.7	3.0	2.3
Malaysia	2.2	1.7	1.4	1.2	1.0	0.9	1.0	1.0	1.0	2.8
Philippines[1]	1.8	1.5	1.5	2.1	1.9	1.9	2.2	2.2	2.2	2.2
Singapore	..	1.3	1.8	2.5	2.5	2.5	2.5	2.5	2.6	2.5
OECD Average[2]	6.6	6.7	6.8	6.4	6.7	6.7	6.8	6.8	7.0	..
Japan[2]	1.9	2.4	2.6	2.6	2.6	2.7	2.7	2.8	3.9	4.4
Korea[2]	3.7	3.7	3.9	4.1	4.1	4.1	4.3	4.1	4.2	3.9

.. Not available

1. The data exclude revenue from VAT on imports. This revenue could not be distinguished from revenue from other import duties and is currently classified under heading 5120 (taxes on specific goods and services).
2. The OECD average represents the unweighted average for OECD member countries. Japan and Korea are also part of the OECD (35) group. Data for Japan, Korea and the OECD average are taken from OECD (2016), Revenue Statistics 2016, *http://dx.doi.org/10.1787/rev_stats-2016-en-fr*, and are preliminary for 2015.

StatLink *http://dx.doi.org/10.1787/888933544113*

Table 3.13. **Taxes on general consumption (5110) as percentage of total taxation**

	1997	2000	2005	2009	2010	2011	2012	2013	2014	2015
Indonesia	35.5	29.4	27.0	29.0	29.6	29.1	31.4	32.3	31.8	31.1
Kazakhstan	..	22.4	17.7	14.3	13.1	12.0	12.4	16.3	14.3	14.8
Malaysia	10.8	11.5	8.8	7.5	6.9	5.9	5.9	6.1	6.2	18.2
Philippines[1]	10.6	9.5	10.2	14.0	13.0	12.5	13.8	13.4	13.2	13.1
Singapore	..	8.3	14.9	18.9	19.6	18.9	18.0	18.6	18.9	18.6
OECD Average[2]	20.1	19.9	20.6	20.1	20.7	20.6	20.5	20.5	20.7	..
Japan[2]	7.2	9.1	9.5	9.6	9.6	9.4	9.2	9.2	12.2	..
Korea[2]	18.9	17.0	17.4	17.2	17.5	17.0	17.2	17.0	17.2	15.3

.. Not available

1. The data exclude revenue from VAT on imports. This revenue could not be distinguished from revenue from other import duties and is currently classified under heading 5120 (taxes on specific goods and services).

2. The OECD average represents the unweighted average for OECD member countries. Japan and Korea are also part of the OECD (35) group. Data for Japan, Korea and the OECD average are taken from OECD (2016), Revenue Statistics 2016, *http://dx.doi.org/10.1787/rev_stats-2016-en-fr*, and are preliminary for 2015.

StatLink ⟐ *http://dx.doi.org/10.1787/888933544132*

Table 3.14. **Taxes on specific goods and services (5120) as percentage of GDP**

	1997	2000	2005	2009	2010	2011	2012	2013	2014	2015
Indonesia	1.1	1.3	1.7	1.3	1.4	1.7	1.7	1.6	1.5	1.6
Kazakhstan	..	2.1	3.9	4.8	8.3	9.8	9.2	8.3	7.7	4.6
Malaysia	5.4	2.9	3.2	2.4	2.4	2.3	2.3	2.2	2.2	1.6
Philippines[1]	6.5	5.0	4.4	4.0	4.1	3.9	3.9	4.1	4.4	4.3
Singapore	..	2.0	1.6	1.4	1.3	1.3	1.2	1.2	1.3	1.4
OECD Average[2]	3.7	3.6	3.4	3.2	3.3	3.3	3.3	3.3	3.3	..
Japan[2]	2.1	2.1	2.1	2.0	2.0	2.0	2.0	2.0	1.9	1.9
Korea[2]	4.2	4.2	3.6	3.2	3.5	2.9	3.0	2.9	2.7	2.8

.. Not available

1. The data include revenues from VAT on imports, usually classified under heading 5110 (taxes on general consumption). This revenue could not be distinguished from revenue from other import duties.

2. The OECD average represents the unweighted average for OECD member countries. Japan and Korea are also part of the OECD (35) group. Data for Japan, Korea and the OECD average are taken from OECD (2016), Revenue Statistics 2016, *http://dx.doi.org/10.1787/rev_stats-2016-en-fr*, and are preliminary for 2015.

StatLink ⟐ *http://dx.doi.org/10.1787/888933544151*

Table 3.15. **Taxes on specific goods and services (5120) as percentage of total taxation**

	1997	2000	2005	2009	2010	2011	2012	2013	2014	2015
Indonesia	12.1	15.3	12.9	11.3	12.2	13.8	13.5	13.1	12.6	13.2
Kazakhstan	..	10.4	15.2	22.5	35.1	39.9	38.8	36.6	36.3	29.5
Malaysia	26.8	19.8	20.0	14.7	16.6	14.4	13.7	13.7	13.6	10.6
Philippines[1]	39.1	32.0	28.9	26.7	27.6	25.6	24.5	25.4	26.2	25.5
Singapore	..	13.0	13.5	10.5	10.3	9.8	8.9	8.9	9.5	10.0
OECD Average[2]	11.5	11.1	10.4	10.1	10.2	10.0	10.0	9.8	9.6	..
Japan[2]	7.9	8.0	7.7	7.3	7.2	7.1	6.9	6.7	6.0	..
Korea[2]	21.6	19.7	15.9	13.6	15.1	12.2	12.0	11.8	10.8	10.9

.. Not available

1. The data include revenues from VAT on imports, usually classified under heading 5110 (taxes on general consumption). This revenue could not be distinguished from revenue from other import duties.

2. The OECD average represents the unweighted average for OECD member countries. Japan and Korea are also part of the OECD (35) group. Data for Japan, Korea and the OECD average are taken from OECD (2016), Revenue Statistics 2016, *http://dx.doi.org/10.1787/rev_stats-2016-en-fr*, and are preliminary for 2015.

StatLink ⟐ *http://dx.doi.org/10.1787/888933544170*

Table 3.16. **Gross domestic product for tax reporting years at market prices, in billions of national currency units**

	1997	2000	2005	2009	2010	2011	2012	2013	2014	2015
Indonesia	627 696	1 389 770	2 774 281	5 606 203	6 864 133	7 831 726	8 615 705	9 546 134	10 569 705	11 531 717
Kazakhstan	1 672	2 600	7 591	17 008	21 816	29 380	31 015	35 999	39 676	40 884
Malaysia	282	356	544	713	821	912	971	1 019	1 107	1 157
Philippines	2 689	3 581	5 678	8 026	9 004	9 708	10 561	11 538	12 645	13 307
Singapore	149	165	212	280	322	347	361	379	390	408
OECD member countries										
Japan	521 295	510 835	505 349	473 996	480 528	474 171	474 404	482 401	489 558	500 535
Korea	530 347	635 185	919 797	1 151 708	1 265 308	1 332 681	1 377 457	1 429 445	1 486 079	1 558 592

Source: National statistical offices, CEIC for Indonesia, Kazakhstan, Malaysia, the Philippines and Singapore and OECD National Accounts data for Japan and Korea.

StatLink ⧉ *http://dx.doi.org/10.1787/888933544189*

Table 3.17. **Gross domestic product for tax reporting years at market prices, in millions of US Dollars at market exchange rates**

	1997	2000	2005	2009	2010	2011	2012	2013	2014	2015
Indonesia	217 906	165 612	285 864	538 639	755 392	892 401	918 104	912 590	890 555	861 256
Kazakhstan	22 166	18 292	57 124	115 309	148 047	200 379	207 999	236 635	221 416	184 388
Malaysia	100 007	93 790	143 536	202 372	255 192	298 180	314 760	323 445	338 234	296 400
Philippines	91 234	81 023	103 074	168 485	199 591	224 143	250 092	271 836	284 830	292 451
Singapore	100 103	95 784	127 436	192 447	236 552	275 729	289 334	302 595	308 169	296 884
OECD member countries										
Japan	4 308 348	4 737 202	4 588 525	5 065 603	5 475 432	5 948 938	5 943 896	4 942 730	4 625 123	4 136 570
Korea	557 962	561 792	898 041	903 338	1 095 096	1 203 539	1 223 389	1 305 518	1 411 196	1 377 689

Note: This table is produced based on GDP data in national currency from Table 3.16 and exchange rate data from Table 3.19.

StatLink ⧉ *http://dx.doi.org/10.1787/888933544208*

Table 3.18. **Total tax revenue in millions of US dollars at market exchange rates**

	1997	2000	2005	2009	2010	2011	2012	2013	2014	2015
Indonesia	19 906	14 264	38 654	63 897	85 782	108 615	114 616	113 930	108 323	101 714
Kazakhstan	..	3 621	14 590	24 445	35 169	49 189	49 614	53 445	46 682	28 652
Malaysia	20 195	13 647	23 122	32 577	36 752	47 192	52 351	52 796	53 634	45 421
Philippines	15 201	12 770	15 678	25 303	29 501	33 928	39 530	44 023	47 563	49 715
Singapore	..	14 857	15 435	25 180	30 709	36 649	40 128	40 885	42 707	40 482
OECD member countries										
Japan	1 152 932	1 262 348	1 252 471	1 365 456	1 509 557	1 702 089	1 748 801	1 500 043	1 482 010	..
Korea	108 274	120 547	202 441	214 634	256 154	290 720	303 158	317 220	347 014	347 878

.. Not available

Note: This table is produced based on total tax revenues from Chapter 4 and exchange rate data from Table 3.19.

StatLink ⧉ *http://dx.doi.org/10.1787/888933544227*

Table 3.19. **Exchange rates used, national currency per US dollar**

	1997	2000	2005	2009	2010	2011	2012	2013	2014	2015
Indonesia	2 880.60	8 391.70	9 704.90	10 408.10	9 086.90	8 776.00	9 384.20	10 460.50	11 868.70	13 389.40
Kazakhstan	75.40	142.10	132.90	147.50	147.40	146.60	149.10	152.10	179.20	221.70
Malaysia	2.80	3.80	3.80	3.50	3.20	3.10	3.10	3.10	3.30	3.90
Philippines	29.50	44.20	55.10	47.60	45.10	43.30	42.20	42.40	44.40	45.50
Singapore	1.50	1.70	1.70	1.50	1.40	1.30	1.20	1.30	1.30	1.40
OECD member countries										
Japan	121.00	107.80	110.10	93.60	87.80	79.70	79.80	97.60	105.80	121.00
Korea	950.50	1 130.60	1 024.20	1 274.90	1 155.40	1 107.30	1 125.90	1 094.90	1 053.10	1 131.30

Source: National statistical offices, and CEIC for Indonesia, Kazakhstan, Malaysia, the Philippines and Singapore and OECD National Accounts data for Japan and Korea.

StatLink ⧉ *http://dx.doi.org/10.1787/888933544246*

3.2. Comparative figures

Figure 3.1. **Tax revenue of main headings as % of total tax revenue, 2015**

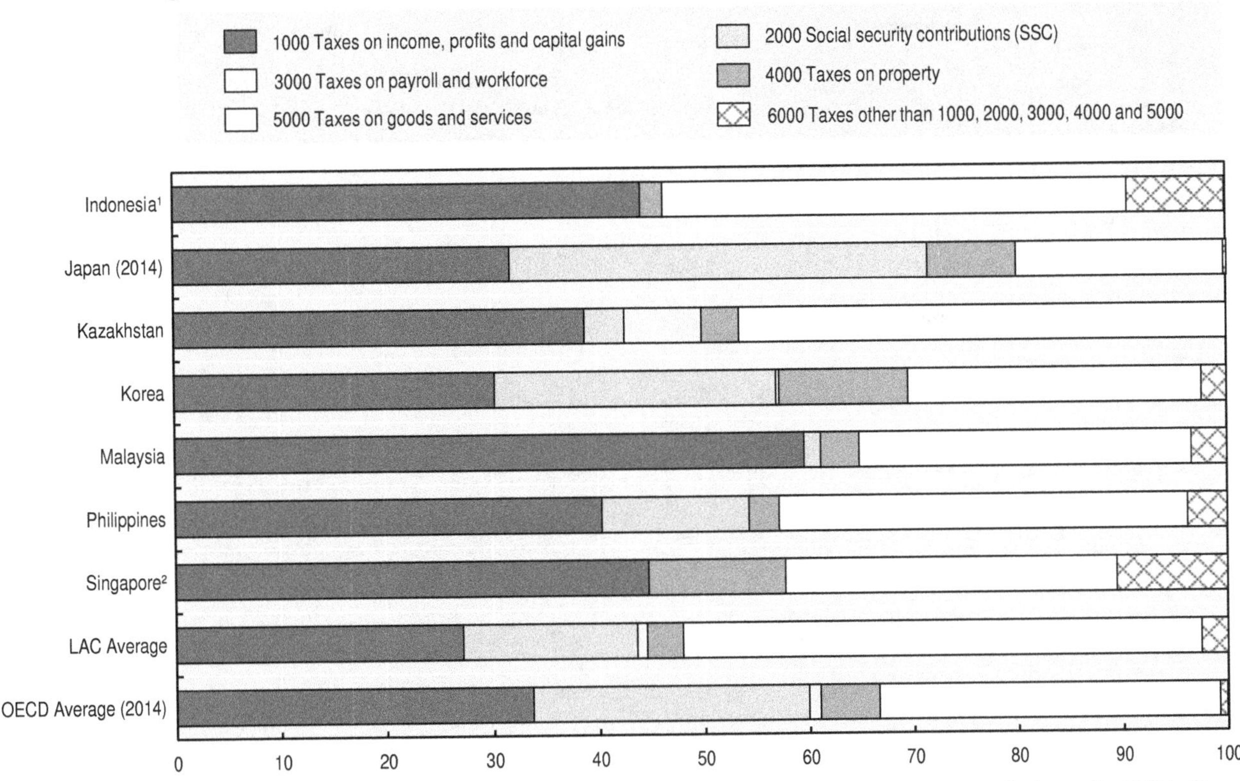

Note: Data for Korea, Japan and the OECD average are taken from *Revenue Statistics* (OECD, 2016a) and are preliminary for 2015 in Korea. Data for 2014 are used for the OECD average and for Japan as data for 2015 are not available.

1. The figures for social security contributions (heading 2000) are not available but they are thought to be negligible as they relate only to the "Asuransi Kesehatan" – a health insurance programme for employees in for-profit state-owned enterprises.

2. There are no social security contributions in Singapore.

Source: Table 3.2.

StatLink ⟦⟧ *http://dx.doi.org/10.1787/888933543790*

Figure 3.2. **Tax structures, 1990-2015**

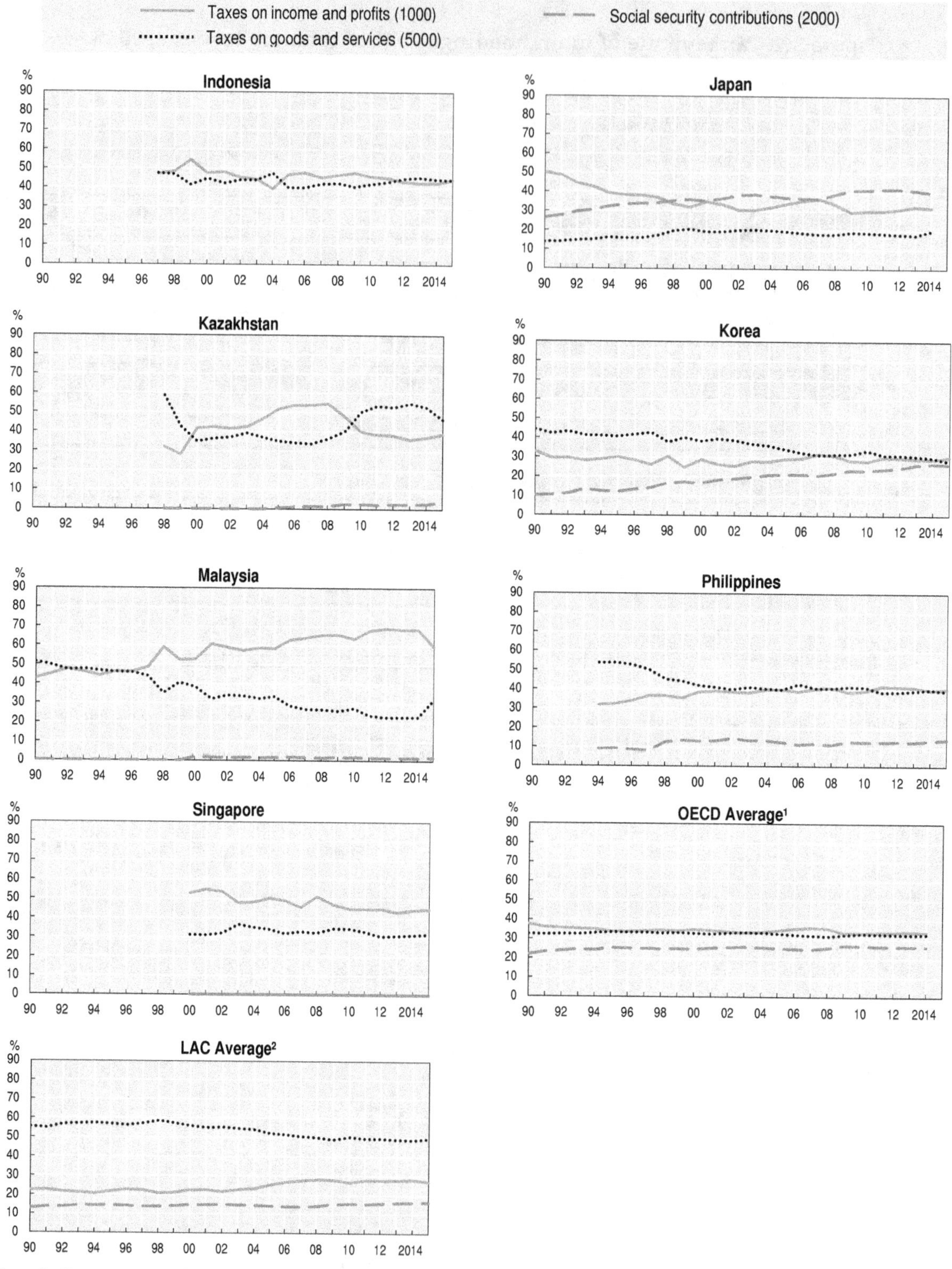

Note: Data for Korea, Japan and the OECD average are taken from *Revenue Statistics* (OECD, 2016a) and are preliminary for 2015 in Korea.
1. Represents the unweighted average for OECD member countries. Japan and Korea are also part of the OECD (35) group.
2. Represents the unweighted average for 24 LAC (Latin American and Caribbean) countries.

Source: OECD.Stats, Revenue Statistics - Asian Countries : Comparative tables.

StatLink ᵄ᷉᷉ *http://dx.doi.org/10.1787/888933543809*

Chapter 4

COUNTRY TABLES,
1997-2015 – Tax revenues

Table 4.1. **Indonesia**

Billion IDR

	1997	2000	2005	2009	2010	2011	2012	2013	2014	2015
Total tax revenue	57 340	119 697	375 136	665 047	779 484	953 206	1 075 584	1 191 766	1 285 655	1 361 889
1000 Taxes on income, profits and capital gains	27 062	57 073	175 541	317 615	357 046	431 122	465 070	506 443	546 181	602 308
1100 Of individuals	..	..	59 733	107 632	122 031	150 537	171 210	197 987	238 058	292 819
1110 On income and profits	..	..	..	..	..	..	..	..	..	..
1120 On capital gains	..	..	..	..	..	..	..	..	..	..
1200 Corporate	..	..	115 808	209 983	235 015	280 585	293 859	308 456	308 123	309 489
1210 On profits	..	..	..	..	..	..	..	..	..	..
1220 On capital gains	..	..	..	..	..	..	..	..	..	..
1300 Unallocable between 1100 and 1200	27 062	57 073	0	0	0	0	0	0	0	0
2000 Social security contributions	..	..	..	..	..	..	..	..	..	..
2100 Employees	..	..	..	..	..	..	..	..	..	..
2110 On a payroll basis	..	..	..	..	..	..	..	..	..	..
2120 On an income tax basis	..	..	..	..	..	..	..	..	..	..
2200 Employers	..	..	..	..	..	..	..	..	..	..
2210 On a payroll basis	..	..	..	..	..	..	..	..	..	..
2220 On an income tax basis	..	..	..	..	..	..	..	..	..	..
2300 Self-employed or non-employed	..	..	..	..	..	..	..	..	..	..
2310 On a payroll basis	..	..	..	..	..	..	..	..	..	..
2320 On an income tax basis	..	..	..	..	..	..	..	..	..	..
2400 Unallocable between 2100, 2200 and 2300	..	..	..	..	..	..	..	..	..	..
2410 On a payroll basis	..	..	..	..	..	..	..	..	..	..
2420 On an income tax basis	..	..	..	..	..	..	..	..	..	..
3000 Taxes on payroll and workforce	0	0	0	0	0	0	0	0	0	0
4000 Taxes on property	2 413	4 456	19 649	30 735	36 607	29 892	28 969	25 305	23 476	29 250
4100 Recurrent taxes on immovable property	2 413	3 525	16 217	24 270	28 581	29 893	28 969	25 305	23 476	29 250
4110 Households	..	..	..	..	..	..	..	..	..	..
4120 Others	..	..	..	..	..	..	..	..	..	..
4200 Recurrent taxes on net wealth	0	0	0	0	0	0	0	0	0	0
4210 Individual	..	..	..	..	..	..	..	..	..	..
4220 Corporate	..	..	..	..	..	..	..	..	..	..
4300 Estate, inheritance and gift taxes	0	0	0	0	0	0	0	0	0	0
4310 Estate and inheritance taxes	..	..	..	..	..	..	..	..	..	..
4320 Gift taxes	..	..	..	..	..	..	..	..	..	..
4400 Taxes on financial and capital transactions	0	931	3 432	6 465	8 026	-1	0	0	0	0
Tax on acquisition of land and buildings	..	931	3 432	6 465	8 026	-1	..	..	..	..
4500 Non-recurrent taxes	0	0	0	0	0	0	0	0	0	0
4510 On net wealth	..	..	..	..	..	..	..	..	..	..
4520 Other non-recurrent taxes	..	..	..	..	..	..	..	..	..	..
4600 Other recurrent taxes on property	0	0	0	0	0	0	0	0	0	0
5000 Taxes on goods and services	27 274	53 547	149 791	268 456	325 685	408 932	482 269	540 622	570 915	603 292
5100 Taxes on production, sale, transfer, etc	27 274	53 547	149 791	268 456	325 685	408 932	482 269	540 622	570 915	603 292
5110 General taxes	20 351	35 232	101 296	193 068	230 605	277 800	337 585	384 714	409 182	423 711
5111 Value added taxes	20 351	35 232	101 296	193 068	230 605	277 800	337 585	384 714	409 182	423 711
5112 Sales tax	0	0	0	0	0	0	0	0	0	0
5113 Other	0	0	0	0	0	0	0	0	0	0
5120 Taxes on specific goods and services	6 923	18 315	48 495	75 389	95 080	131 131	144 684	155 909	161 734	179 581
5121 Excises	4 263	11 287	33 256	56 718	66 166	77 010	95 028	108 452	118 086	144 641
5122 Profits of fiscal monopolies	0	0	0	0	0	0	0	0	0	0
5123 Customs and import duties	2 579	6 697	14 921	18 105	20 017	25 266	28 418	31 621	32 319	31 213
5124 Taxes on exports	81	331	318	565	8 898	28 856	21 238	15 835	11 329	3 727
5125 Taxes on investment goods	0	0	0	0	0	0	0	0	0	0
5126 Taxes on specific services	0	0	0	0	0	0	0	0	0	0
5127 Other taxes on internat. trade and transactions	0	0	0	0	0	0	0	0	0	0
5128 Other taxes	0	0	0	0	0	0	0	0	0	0
5130 Unallocable between 5110 and 5120	0	0	0	0	0	0	0	0	0	0
5200 Taxes on use of goods and to perform activities	0	0	0	0	0	0	0	0	0	0
5210 Recurrent taxes	..	..	..	..	..	..	..	..	..	..
5211 Paid by households: motor vehicles	..	..	..	..	..	..	..	..	..	..
5212 Paid by others: motor vehicles	..	..	..	..	..	..	..	..	..	..
5213 Paid in respect of other goods	..	..	..	..	..	..	..	..	..	..
5220 Non-recurrent taxes	..	..	..	..	..	..	..	..	..	..
5300 Unallocable between 5100 and 5200	0	0	0	0	0	0	0	0	0	0
6000 Other taxes	591	4 621	30 155	48 241	60 146	83 260	99 276	119 397	145 082	127 038
6100 Paid solely by business	0	0	0	0	0	0	0	0	0	0

Table 4.1. **Indonesia** (*cont.*)

Billion IDR

	1997	2000	2005	2009	2010	2011	2012	2013	2014	2015
6200 Other	591	4 621	30 155	48 241	60 146	83 260	99 276	119 397	145 082	127 038
Other local level	0	3 784	28 105	45 125	56 177	79 332	95 066	114 460	138 789	121 470
Other non local level	591	837	2 050	3 116	3 969	3 928	4 211	4 937	6 293	5 568

Note:

Year ending 31st December.

The data are on a cash basis.

The figures for social security contributions (heading 2000) are not available but they are thought to be negligible as they relate only to the "Asuransi Kesehatan" - a health insurance programme for employees in for-profit state-owned enterprises.

Source: Ministry of Finance of the Republic of Indonesia.

StatLink ᴍᴤ᾽ *http://dx.doi.org/10.1787/888933544265*

Table 4.2. **Japan**

Billion JPY

	1997	2000	2005	2009	2010	2011	2012	2013	2014	2015
Total tax revenue	**139 501**	**136 125**	**137 939**	**127 768**	**132 480**	**135 668**	**139 578**	**146 401**	**156 867**	..
1000 Taxes on income, profits and capital gains	**51 673**	**47 398**	**46 631**	**37 739**	**40 034**	**40 910**	**43 352**	**47 534**	**49 939**	**51 870**
1100 Of individuals	29 809	28 677	25 222	25 518	24 663	24 951	25 946	28 150	29 655	30 541
1110 On income and profits	29 809	28 677	25 222	25 518	24 663	24 951	25 946	28 150	29 655	30 541
Income tax	19 183	18 789	16 702	12 914	12 984	13 476	14 044	15 865	17 139	17 958
Prefectural inhabitants tax	3 183	3 621	2 606	5 052	4 699	4 608	4 783	5 090	5 215	5 265
Municipal inhabitants tax	7 172	6 044	5 699	7 349	6 795	6 688	6 942	7 015	7 114	7 126
Enterprise tax	271	223	216	204	184	179	178	181	186	192
1120 On capital gains	0	0	0	0	0	0	0	0	0	0
1200 Corporate	21 864	18 721	21 408	12 221	15 372	15 959	17 406	19 384	20 284	21 329
1210 On profits	21 864	18 721	21 408	12 221	15 372	15 959	17 406	19 384	20 284	21 329
Corporation tax	13 477	11 747	13 274	6 356	8 968	9 351	10 408	11 698	11 464	11 741
Prefectural inhabitants tax	1 026	879	979	715	777	800	846	854	963	866
Municipal inhabitants tax	2 532	2 176	2 457	1 775	1 954	2 011	2 129	2 157	2 445	2 348
Enterprise tax	4 830	3 918	4 698	2 701	2 253	2 240	2 354	2 674	3 017	3 677
Local special corporate tax	0	0	0	674	1 420	1 556	1 670	2 001	2 395	2 175
Local corporate tax	0	0	0	0	0	0	0	0	1	523
1220 On capital gains	0	0	0	0	0	0	0	0	0	0
1300 Unallocable between 1100 and 1200	0	0	0	0	0	0	0	0	0	0
2000 Social security contributions	**47 744**	**47 857**	**50 844**	**52 342**	**54 456**	**56 321**	**58 068**	**59 800**	**62 232**	..
2100 Employees	19 642	19 786	20 980	22 484	23 590	24 431	25 182	25 982	27 146	..
2110 On a payroll basis	19 642	19 786	20 980	22 484	23 590	24 431	25 182	25 982	27 146	..
2120 On an income tax basis	0	0	0	0	0	0	0	0	0	..
2200 Employers	22 750	22 388	23 151	23 575	24 672	25 735	26 333	27 141	28 394	..
2210 On a payroll basis	22 750	22 388	23 151	23 575	24 672	25 735	26 333	27 141	28 394	..
2220 On an income tax basis	0	0	0	0	0	0	0	0	0	..
2300 Self-employed or non-employed	5 352	5 683	6 712	6 282	6 194	6 156	6 553	6 676	6 693	..
2310 On a payroll basis	5 352	5 683	6 712	6 282	6 194	6 156	6 553	6 676	6 693	..
2320 On an income tax basis	0	0	0	0	0	0	0	0	0	..
2400 Unallocable between 2100, 2200 and 2300	0	0	0	0	0	0	0	0	0	..
2410 On a payroll basis	..	..	..	..	..	..	..	..	..	..
2420 On an income tax basis	..	..	..	..	..	..	..	..	..	..
3000 Taxes on payroll and workforce	**0**	**0**	**0**	**0**	**0**	**0**	**0**	**0**	**0**	**0**
4000 Taxes on property	**15 679**	**14 294**	**13 327**	**12 949**	**12 878**	**13 100**	**12 716**	**12 940**	**13 306**	**13 050**
4100 Recurrent taxes on immovable property	10 410	10 414	10 116	10 128	10 225	10 237	9 799	9 882	10 016	9 900
Prefectural property tax	8	11	16	19	5	3	2	2	2	2
Municipal property tax	8 822	9 041	8 862	8 874	8 961	8 966	8 580	8 653	8 769	8 666
City planning tax	1 326	1 318	1 233	1 233	1 256	1 268	1 216	1 227	1 244	1 230
Special landholding tax	94	43	4	2	3	1	1	1	2	3
Water and land utilisation tax	0	0	0	0	0	0	0	0	0	0
Land value tax	160	1	0	0	0	0	0	0	0	0
4110 Households	..	..	..	..	..	..	..	..	..	..
4120 Others	..	..	..	..	..	..	..	..	..	..
4200 Recurrent taxes on net wealth	0	0	0	0	0	0	0	0	0	0
4210 Individual	..	..	..	..	..	..	..	..	..	..
4220 Corporate	..	..	..	..	..	..	..	..	..	..
4300 Estate, inheritance and gift taxes	2 413	1 782	1 566	1 350	1 250	1 474	1 504	1 574	1 883	1 761
4310 Estate and inheritance taxes	..	..	..	..	..	..	..	..	..	..
Inheritance tax	..	..	..	..	..	..	..	..	..	..
4320 Gift taxes	..	..	..	..	..	..	..	..	..	..
Tax on gifts	..	..	..	..	..	..	..	..	..	..
4400 Taxes on financial and capital transactions	2 856	2 099	1 646	1 472	1 403	1 388	1 413	1 483	1 407	1 389
Bourse tax	40	0	0	0	0	0	0	0	0	0
Securities transaction	404	0	0	0	0	0	0	0	0	0
Bank of Japan note issue tax	0	0	0	0	0	0	0	0	0	0
Stamp revenues	1 681	1 532	1 169	1 068	1 024	1 047	1 078	1 126	1 035	1 027
Real property acquisition tax	731	567	477	404	379	342	336	357	372	362
4500 Non-recurrent taxes	0	0	0	0	0	0	0	0	0	0
4510 On net wealth	..	..	..	..	..	..	..	..	..	..
4520 Other non-recurrent taxes	..	..	..	..	..	..	..	..	..	..
4600 Other recurrent taxes on property	0	0	0	0	0	0	0	0	0	0
5000 Taxes on goods and services	**24 058**	**26 227**	**26 786**	**24 364**	**24 730**	**24 966**	**25 056**	**25 744**	**30 991**	**33 819**
5100 Taxes on production, sale, transfer, etc	21 132	23 180	23 722	21 561	22 160	22 410	22 592	23 313	28 587	31 417
5110 General taxes	10 112	12 350	13 135	12 221	12 675	12 745	12 902	13 479	19 135	21 984

Table 4.2. **Japan** (cont.)

Billion JPY

	1997	2000	2005	2009	2010	2011	2012	2013	2014	2015
5111 Value added taxes	10 112	12 350	13 135	12 221	12 675	12 745	12 902	13 479	19 135	21 984
5112 Sales tax	0	0	0	0	0	0	0	0	0	0
5113 Other	0	0	0	0	0	0	0	0	0	0
5120 Taxes on specific goods and services	11 021	10 830	10 588	9 340	9 485	9 665	9 690	9 834	9 452	9 433
5121 Excises	9 764	9 837	9 571	8 527	8 622	8 719	8 721	8 728	8 308	8 248
Liquor tax	1 962	1 816	1 585	1 417	1 389	1 369	1 350	1 371	1 328	1 308
Sugar excises	0	0	0	0	0	0	0	0	0	0
Local gasoline tax	276	296	311	291	294	283	281	275	266	264
Gasoline tax	2 583	2 769	2 908	2 715	2 750	2 648	2 622	2 574	2 486	2 466
Liquefied petroleum gas tax	29	28	29	25	24	23	21	21	19	20
Aviation fuel tax	104	104	105	94	89	60	64	67	67	66
Commodity tax	0	0	0	0	0	0	0	0	0	0
Playing-card tax	0	0	0	0	0	0	0	0	0	0
Prefectural tobacco tax	248	282	275	250	256	293	289	173	155	152
Municipal tobacco tax	799	865	845	767	788	900	887	983	950	928
Timber delivery tax	0	0	0	0	0	0	0	0	0	0
Mineral product tax	2	2	2	2	2	2	2	2	2	2
Electricity and gas tax	0	0	0	0	0	0	0	0	0	0
Diesel oil tax	1 331	1 208	1 086	908	918	932	925	943	936	924
Vehicle acquisition tax	562	464	453	231	192	168	210	193	86	122
Promotion of power resources development tax	354	375	359	329	349	331	328	328	321	323
Petroleum and coal tax	497	489	493	487	502	519	567	600	631	628
Tobacco tax	1 018	876	887	822	908	1 032	1 018	1 038	919	906
Special tobacco tax	0	264	233	190	163	160	158	161	142	140
5122 Profits of fiscal monopolies	0	0	0	0	0	0	0	0	0	0
Monopoly profits	..	..	..	..	..	..	..	..	..	..
5123 Customs and import duties	1 012	877	930	732	786	874	897	1 034	1 073	1 117
Customs duty	1 012	877	930	732	786	874	897	1 034	1 073	1 117
5124 Taxes on exports	0	0	0	0	0	0	0	0	0	0
5125 Taxes on investment goods	0	0	0	0	0	0	0	0	0	0
5126 Taxes on specific services	245	116	87	81	77	72	73	71	70	68
Travel tax	0	0	0	0	0	0	0	0	0	0
Admission tax	0	0	0	0	0	0	0	0	0	0
Local entertainment tax	0	0	0	0	0	0	0	0	0	0
Golf course utilisation tax	98	81	62	58	55	51	51	49	48	46
Meal and lodging tax	0	0	0	0	0	0	0	0	0	0
Special local consumption tax	125	12	0	0	0	0	0	0	0	0
Bathing tax	22	23	24	23	22	21	22	22	22	22
5127 Other taxes on internat. trade and transactions	0	0	0	0	0	0	0	0	0	0
5128 Other taxes	0	0	0	0	0	0	0	0	0	0
5130 Unallocable between 5110 and 5120	0	0	0	0	0	0	0	0	0	0
5200 Taxes on use of goods and to perform activities	2 926	3 047	3 064	2 803	2 570	2 557	2 464	2 431	2 404	2 402
5210 Recurrent taxes	2 905	3 027	3 043	2 783	2 548	2 535	2 442	2 409	2 382	2 380
Automobile tax	1 705	1 765	1 753	1 654	1 616	1 597	1 586	1 574	1 556	1 535
Light vehicle tax	113	125	152	174	178	180	184	189	195	213
Motor vehicle tonnage tax	1 084	1 134	1 136	953	753	755	669	643	629	631
Hunter licence tax	2	2	0	0	0	0	0	0	0	0
Hunting tax	1	1	3	2	2	2	2	2	2	1
Mine lot tax	1	1	0	0	0	0	0	0	0	0
5211 Paid by households: motor vehicles	..	..	..	..	..	..	..	..	..	..
5212 Paid by others: motor vehicles	..	..	..	..	..	..	..	..	..	..
5213 Paid in respect of other goods	..	..	..	..	..	..	..	..	..	..
5220 Non-recurrent taxes	21	20	21	20	21	22	22	22	23	23
5300 Unallocable between 5100 and 5200	0	0	0	0	0	0	0	0	0	0
6000 Other taxes	**346**	**348**	**351**	**374**	**381**	**371**	**386**	**384**	**399**	**406**
6100 Paid solely by business	325	324	297	328	330	339	350	348	356	356
Business office tax	325	324	297	328	330	339	350	348	356	356
6200 Other	22	24	54	46	52	32	36	36	43	50
Taxes not in local tax law	21	24	54	46	52	32	36	36	43	50
Other	0	0	0	0	0	0	0	0	0	0

Table 4.2. **Japan** *(cont.)*

Note:

Figures are taken from OECD (2016), *Revenue Statistics 2016*, *http://dx.doi.org/10.1787/rev_stats-2016-en-fr*, and are preliminary for 2015. Data are on a fiscal year basis beginning 1st April.

From 1990, data are on an accrual basis.

The figures for different groups of taxes are reported on different reporting bases, namely: Social security contributions (heading 2000) : in principle accrual basis, Central government taxes : accrual basis (revenues accrued during the fiscal year plus cash receipts collected before the end of May (the end of April until 1977), Local government taxes : accrual basis (due to be paid during the fiscal year and cash receipts collected before the end of May).

The Japanese authorities take the view that the Enterprise tax (classified in 1100 and 1200) and the Mineral product tax (classified in 5121) should be classified in heading 6000 since under articles 72 and 519 of the Local Tax Law these taxes are regarded as levies on the business or mining activity itself.

Heading 2000: Includes some unidentifiable voluntary contributions. Preliminary data for 2015 were not available at the time OECD (2016), Revenue Statistics 2016 was prepared.

Heading 2300: Includes contributions to the National pension, National Health Insurance and the Farmer's pension fund. Contributions to the

Farmer's pension fund are not available for the years before 1999.

Heading 4100: Municipal property tax, includes Prefectural property tax from 1990 to 1994 because data are not available to provide a breakdown.

Heading 5121: Municipal tobacco tax, includes Prefectural tobacco tax from 1990 to 1994 because data are not available to provide a breakdown.

Heading 5121: In sub-item Petroleum and coal tax, the data before 2003 refer to petroleum tax.

Source: Tax Bureau, Ministry of Finance.

StatLink *http://dx.doi.org/10.1787/888933544284*

Table 4.3. **Kazakhstan**

Million KZT

	1997	2000	2005	2009	2010	2011	2012	2013	2014	2015
Total tax revenue	..	**514 722**	**1 938 689**	**3 605 585**	**5 182 314**	**7 212 132**	**7 398 056**	**8 130 544**	**8 364 983**	**6 352 921**
1000 Taxes on income, profits and capital gains	..	**214 545**	**1 001 587**	**1 726 005**	**2 072 357**	**2 774 181**	**2 826 237**	**2 928 127**	**3 113 992**	**2 467 977**
1100 Of individuals	..	51 016	122 999	268 725	312 332	376 245	438 498	492 991	552 280	598 807
1110 On income and profits	..	51 016	122 999	268 725	312 332	376 245	438 498	492 991	552 280	598 807
From non-foreign citizens	..	51 016	122 999	240 265	276 089	336 185	395 988	442 561	492 913	566 974
From foreign citizens	..	0	0	28 460	36 243	40 060	42 509	50 430	59 367	31 832
1120 On capital gains	..	..	..	..	..	..	..	..	..	..
1200 Corporate	..	163 529	878 588	1 457 280	1 760 025	2 397 936	2 387 739	2 435 136	2 561 712	1 869 170
1210 On profits	..	163 529	878 588	1 457 280	1 760 025	2 397 936	2 387 739	2 435 136	2 561 712	1 869 170
From non-oil companies	..	163 529	508 771	664 480	847 057	1 094 909	1 052 499	1 039 044	1 172 635	1 236 561
From oil companies	..	0	369 817	0	0	0	0	0	0	0
From oil companies to National Fund	..	0	0	792 800	912 968	1 303 027	1 335 241	1 396 092	1 389 077	632 609
1220 On capital gains	..	..	..	..	..	..	..	..	..	..
1300 Unallocable between 1100 and 1200	..	0	0	0	0	0	0	0	0	0
2000 Social security contributions	..	**0**	**13 758**	**89 446**	**131 041**	**157 105**	**183 225**	**203 361**	**225 948**	**240 590**
2100 Employees	..	..	..	..	..	..	..	..	..	..
2110 On a payroll basis	..	..	..	..	..	..	..	..	..	..
2120 On an income tax basis	..	..	..	..	..	..	..	..	..	..
2200 Employers	..	..	..	..	..	..	..	..	..	..
2210 On a payroll basis	..	..	..	..	..	..	..	..	..	..
2220 On an income tax basis	..	..	..	..	..	..	..	..	..	..
2300 Self-employed or non-employed	..	..	..	..	..	..	..	..	..	..
2310 On a payroll basis	..	..	..	..	..	..	..	..	..	..
2320 On an income tax basis	..	..	..	..	..	..	..	..	..	..
2400 Unallocable between 2100, 2200 and 2300	..	..	13 758	89 446	131 041	157 105	183 225	203 361	225 948	240 590
2410 On a payroll basis	..	..	..	..	..	..	..	..	..	..
2420 On an income tax basis	..	..	..	..	..	..	..	..	..	..
3000 Taxes on payroll and workforce	..	**99 082**	**197 300**	**232 840**	**253 830**	**296 843**	**340 997**	**380 477**	**427 985**	**464 674**
The social tax	..	99 082	197 300	232 840	253 830	296 843	340 997	380 477	427 985	464 674
4000 Taxes on property	..	**21 013**	**45 996**	**107 366**	**124 632**	**134 109**	**144 757**	**160 845**	**192 063**	**226 853**
4100 Recurrent taxes on immovable property	..	20 504	44 526	105 451	122 146	131 194	141 344	157 424	188 331	224 752
4110 Households	..	3 230	2 865	4 053	4 402	4 919	5 577	6 153	9 385	10 164
4120 Others	..	17 274	41 661	101 399	117 744	126 275	135 767	151 271	178 946	214 588
Uniform land tax	..	235	351	578	762	818	820	830	876	833
Property tax	..	13 699	35 157	88 945	104 745	113 842	123 461	138 015	165 795	200 710
Land tax	..	3 340	6 153	11 876	12 238	11 615	11 486	12 426	12 275	13 045
4200 Recurrent taxes on net wealth	..	0	0	0	0	0	0	0	0	0
4210 Individual	..	..	..	..	..	..	..	..	..	..
4220 Corporate	..	..	..	..	..	..	..	..	..	..
4300 Estate, inheritance and gift taxes	..	0	0	0	0	0	0	0	0	0
4310 Estate and inheritance taxes	..	..	..	..	..	..	..	..	..	..
4320 Gift taxes	..	..	..	..	..	..	..	..	..	..
4400 Taxes on financial and capital transactions	..	509	1 470	1 914	2 486	2 915	3 413	3 421	3 732	2 101
4500 Non-recurrent taxes	..	0	0	0	0	0	0	0	0	0
4510 On net wealth	..	..	..	..	..	..	..	..	..	..
4520 Other non-recurrent taxes	..	..	..	..	..	..	..	..	..	..
4600 Other recurrent taxes on property	..	0	0	0	0	0	0	0	0	0
5000 Taxes on goods and services	..	**179 452**	**680 010**	**1 449 914**	**2 600 449**	**3 849 891**	**3 902 837**	**4 457 631**	**4 404 920**	**2 952 686**
5100 Taxes on production, sale, transfer, etc	..	168 678	637 765	1 327 634	2 497 709	3 740 606	3 782 126	4 300 462	4 237 236	2 816 629
5110 General taxes	..	115 159	343 926	515 933	677 229	865 087	914 194	1 327 433	1 197 258	943 051
5111 Value added taxes	..	115 159	343 926	515 933	677 229	865 087	914 194	1 327 433	1 197 258	943 051
Domestic VAT	..	75 625	68 319	71 409	197 358	208 652	134 144	445 876	333 943	203 247
VAT on imported goods	..	39 534	255 621	404 655	435 869	607 850	723 304	819 129	789 302	667 404
Other VAT	..	0	19 986	39 869	44 002	48 585	56 746	62 428	74 013	72 399
5112 Sales tax	..	0	0	0	0	0	0	0	0	0
5113 Other	..	0	0	0	0	0	0	0	0	0
5120 Taxes on specific goods and services	..	53 519	293 839	811 701	1 820 480	2 875 519	2 867 932	2 973 029	3 039 978	1 873 579
5121 Excises	..	19 285	33 416	57 393	61 423	76 400	93 143	103 651	147 057	161 068
Alcohol	..	12 939	9 821	15 590	15 691	24 098	29 493	29 659	38 788	36 345
Tobacco	..	5 182	5 976	17 961	22 903	29 400	37 700	45 644	78 695	98 346
Petroleum product	..	1 164	14 962	20 530	20 966	20 790	22 599	24 139	25 221	26 216
Automobiles	..	0	2 636	3 312	1 864	2 111	3 351	4 208	4 352	931
Others	..	0	21	0	0	1	0	2	0	-770
5122 Profits of fiscal monopolies	..	0	0	0	0	0	0	0	0	0

Table 4.3. **Kazakhstan** (cont.)

Million KZT

	1997	2000	2005	2009	2010	2011	2012	2013	2014	2015
5123 Customs and import duties	..	18 471	62 249	152 226	354 487	322 316	314 994	297 959	279 313	189 522
5124 Taxes on exports	..	0	940	205 601	492 870	1 323 625	1 264 458	1 466 254	1 513 573	920 175
Taxes on exports	..	..	940	1 243	22 060	499 207	457 410	585 857	778 853	692 855
Taxes on exports to National Fund	..	..	0	204 358	470 810	824 418	807 048	880 397	734 720	227 320
5125 Taxes on investment goods	..	0	0	0	0	0	0	0	0	0
5126 Taxes on specific services	..	0	5 149	10 789	14 566	16 451	16 770	18 862	21 036	24 798
Telecommunication	..	..	3 890	5 167	5 535	5 881	5 309	5 476	6 167	8 151
Placement of outdoor advertisements	..	..	1 259	3 247	3 723	4 664	5 016	5 652	5 981	6 076
Gambling business	..	..	0	1 156	3 693	4 393	5 064	6 385	7 598	9 231
Others	..	..	0	1 219	1 614	1 513	1 381	1 350	1 291	1 340
5127 Other taxes on internat. trade and transactions	..	0	0	0	0	0	0	0	0	0
5128 Other taxes	..	15 763	192 086	385 691	897 133	1 136 727	1 178 567	1 086 303	1 078 999	578 015
Production of useful minerals of non-oil sector companies	..	15 763	108 453	68 618	122 128	148 494	159 313	168 186	122 909	118 073
Production of useful minerals of oil sector companies	..	0	83 633	0	0	0	0	0	0	0
Production of useful minerals of oil sector co. to National Fund	..	0	0	317 073	775 005	988 233	1 019 253	918 117	956 090	459 942
5130 Unallocable between 5110 and 5120	..	0	0	0	0	0	0	0	0	0
5200 Taxes on use of goods and perform activities	..	10 774	42 245	122 280	102 740	109 285	120 711	157 169	167 683	136 057
5210 Recurrent taxes	..	5 901	7 076	17 521	26 262	29 975	30 961	36 029	38 844	42 278
5211 Paid by households: motor vehicles	..	3 930	4 877	13 394	21 565	24 631	25 172	29 629	31 656	34 466
5212 Paid by others: motor vehicles	..	1 971	2 199	4 128	4 697	5 344	5 789	6 401	7 188	7 812
5213 Paid in respect of other goods	..	0	0	0	0	0	0	0	0	0
5220 Non-recurrent taxes	..	4 873	35 169	104 758	76 478	79 310	89 750	121 140	128 840	93 779
Emissions into the environment	..	0	25 523	85 953	57 982	58 466	67 183	93 179	97 712	63 379
Others	..	4 873	9 646	18 805	18 497	20 843	22 567	27 960	31 128	30 399
5300 Unallocable between 5100 and 5200	..	0	0	0	0	0	0	0	0	0
6000 Other taxes	..	**629**	**37**	**15**	**6**	**4**	**3**	**103**	**75**	**141**
6100 Paid solely by business	..	0	0	0	0	0	0	0	0	0
6200 Other	..	629	37	15	6	4	3	103	75	141

Note:

Year ending 31st December.

Data are on a cash basis.

The share of the Republic of Kazakhstan under production sharing contracts of oil companies, the bonuses of oil and non-oil sector companies, the levy for the use of the radio-frequency spectrum, the payment to compensate for historic costs as well as certain other items are classified as non-tax revenues according to the OECD Interpretative Guide, but are considered as tax revenues in Kazakhstan.

Headings 1210, 5124 and 5128: These categories includes revenues that are paid to the National Fund of the Republic of Kazakhstan. This fund was created in 2000 as a stabilisation fund and includes revenues levied from oil and gas companies.

Heading 2000: Social security contribution revenues are not considered as tax revenues in Kazakhstan, but are considered as tax revenues under the OECD Interpretative Guide, subject to certain criteria.

Heading 4120: The uniform land tax is a presumptive tax for farmers and peasants' households. Such payers are not obliged to pay personal income tax, land tax, environmental fees, transport tax, property tax and other mandatory payments to the budget. The uniform land tax is levied on the value of land in use.

Source: Ministry of Finance of the Republic of Kazakhstan.

StatLink http://dx.doi.org/10.1787/888933544303

Table 4.4. **Korea**

Billion KRW

	1997	2000	2005	2009	2010	2011	2012	2013	2014	2015
Total tax revenue	**102 916**	**136 295**	**207 345**	**273 647**	**295 968**	**321 915**	**341 336**	**347 332**	**365 428**	**393 558**
1000 Taxes on income, profits and capital gains	**26 916**	**39 254**	**60 609**	**77 897**	**82 905**	**96 845**	**101 944**	**101 792**	**106 353**	**119 150**
1100 Of individuals	16 543	19 950	27 570	38 618	42 098	47 299	51 185	53 311	59 457	68 625
Income tax	0	0	0	0	0	0	0	0	0	0
Dividends and interest income tax	0	0	3 127	4 762	4 425	4 896	5 152	4 889	4 628	4 561
Wages and salaries income tax	0	0	10 382	13 407	15 517	18 337	19 627	21 931	25 359	27 055
Other income tax	0	0	2 082	2 829	2 986	3 365	3 595	3 432	3 805	4 467
Global income tax	12 911	16 128	4 607	6 117	6 369	8 300	9 938	10 901	11 486	12 784
Defence tax on income tax	0	0	0	0	0	0	0	0	0	0
Education tax on income tax	0	0	0	0	0	0	0	0	0	0
Rural development tax on interest, bus. Inc. & cap.gains relief	149	156	116	199	179	156	125	124	115	105
Inhabitant tax on income tax (local)	1 526	2 285	2 804	3 996	4 459	4 856	5 293	5 377	6 017	7 797
1110 On income and profits	14 586	18 569	23 118	31 310	33 935	39 910	43 730	46 654	51 410	56 769
1120 On capital gains	1 957	1 381	4 452	7 308	8 163	7 389	7 455	6 657	8 047	11 856
Capital gains tax	1 957	1 381	4 452	7 308	8 163	7 389	7 455	6 657	8 047	11 856
1200 Corporate	10 158	19 271	33 039	39 279	40 807	49 546	50 759	48 481	46 896	50 525
Corporation tax - withholding	5 501	8 577	5 682	4 681	9 095	10 534	11 516	12 176	12 172	12 317
Corporation tax - final returns	3 924	9 302	24 123	30 570	28 173	34 339	34 416	31 679	30 478	32 713
Defence tax on corporation tax	0	0	0	0	0	0	0	0	0	0
Inhabitant tax on corporation tax (local)	733	1 142	2 696	3 556	3 094	3 953	4 258	4 118	3 882	5 191
Rural development tax corporate income	0	251	538	472	445	720	569	508	364	304
1210 On profits	10 158	19 271	33 039	39 279	40 807	49 546	50 759	48 481	46 896	50 525
Excess profit tax	0	0	0	0	0	0	0	0	0	0
1220 On capital gains	0	0	0	0	0	0	0	0	0	0
Capital gains tax	..	..	..	..	..	..	..	..	..	..
1300 Unallocable between 1100 and 1200	215	33	0	0	0	0	0	0	0	0
Business income tax	0	0	..	..	..	..	..	..	..	..
Real estate income tax	0	0	..	..	..	..	..	..	..	..
Defence tax on real estate & business income	0	0	..	..	..	..	..	..	..	..
Rural dev. tax on bus. inc. & cap. gains relief	211	30	..	..	..	..	..	..	..	..
Inhabitant tax before 1990 (local)	1	0	..	..	..	..	..	..	..	..
Farm land tax (local)	3	3	..	..	..	..	..	..	..	..
Inhabitant tax on farm land tax (local)	0	0	..	..	..	..	..	..	..	..
2000 Social security contributions	**14 583**	**22 759**	**43 902**	**63 939**	**69 090**	**77 234**	**84 380**	**91 596**	**98 184**	**104 693**
2100 Employees	6 376	8 578	17 632	25 638	28 213	31 875	35 670	38 396	41 355	44 281
Veterans' relief fund	0	0	0	0	0	0	0	0	0	0
Soldiers' annuity fund	0	0	0	0	0	0	0	0	0	0
Unemployment insurance	264	598	1 016	1 346	1 358	1 698	2 138	2 418	2 866	3 076
National welfare pension fund	3 597	4 325	7 746	10 358	11 004	11 832	12 867	13 890	14 823	15 821
Social benefit fund	0	0	0	0	0	0	0	0	0	0
Health insurance	1 149	2 066	6 060	10 581	11 783	13 954	15 718	17 128	18 492	19 868
Teachers' pensions	219	279	520	621	868	940	1 229	1 077	1 081	1 125
Government employees' pensions	1 013	1 144	2 004	2 308	2 878	3 106	3 345	3 435	3 593	3 876
Military personal pensions	134	166	286	313	322	345	373	448	500	515
2110 On a payroll basis	..	8 578	17 632	25 638	28 213	31 875	35 670	38 396	41 355	44 281
2120 On an income tax basis	..	0	0	0	0	0	0	0	0	0
2200 Employers	5 901	9 409	18 486	28 981	30 856	34 366	36 911	41 518	44 806	47 846
Ind. works' insurance fund	1 819	1 876	3 182	4 732	4 632	4 632	5 508	5 436	5 797	6 062
Soldiers' annuity fund	0	0	0	0	0	0	0	0	0	0
Pneumoconiosis fund	0	0	0	0	0	0	0	0	0	0
Unemployment insurance	653	1 449	2 164	2 843	2 860	3 347	4 166	4 545	5 150	5 499
Veterans' relief fund	0	0	0	0	0	0	0	0	0	0
National welfare pension fund	1 814	4 340	7 759	10 393	11 052	11 833	12 930	13 958	14 909	15 895
Social benefit fund	0	0	0	0	0	0	0	0	0	0
Health insurance	1 459	1 547	4 997	8 980	11 718	13 889	13 576	16 826	18 133	19 493
Teachers' pensions	156	197	384	456	594	665	731	753	0	0
Government employees' pensions	0	0	0	0	0	0	0	0	817	897
2210 On a payroll basis	..	9 409	18 486	28 981	30 856	34 366	36 911	41 518	44 806	47 846
2220 On an income tax basis	..	0	0	0	0	0	0	0	0	0
2300 Self-employed or non-employed	2 306	4 772	7 784	9 320	10 021	10 993	11 799	11 682	12 023	12 566
2310 On a payroll basis	0	0	0	0	0	0	0	0	0	0
2320 On an income tax basis	2 306	4 772	7 784	9 234	10 021	10 993	11 799	11 682	12 023	12 566
2400 Unallocable between 2100, 2200 and 2300	0	0	0	0	0	0	0	0	0	0
2410 On a payroll basis	..	..	..	..	..	..	..	..	..	..

Table 4.4. **Korea** (cont.)

Billion KRW

	1997	2000	2005	2009	2010	2011	2012	2013	2014	2015
2420 On an income tax basis	..	..	..	..	..	..	..	..	..	..
3000 Taxes on payroll and workforce	**309**	**258**	**514**	**681**	**714**	**803**	**868**	**981**	**1 042**	**1 122**
Workshop tax on workforce (local)	309	258	514	681	714	803	868	981	1 042	1 122
Vocational training promotion fund	0	0	0	0	0	0	0	0	0	0
4000 Taxes on property	**13 088**	**16 846**	**24 697**	**31 803**	**33 516**	**36 555**	**36 213**	**35 847**	**40 305**	**48 625**
4100 Recurrent taxes on immovable property	2 986	3 385	5 030	8 859	9 270	9 779	10 315	10 809	11 654	12 486
Property tax (local)	577	728	2 588	4 423	4 817	7 617	8 049	8 267	8 780	9 294
City planning tax on urban real estate (local)	731	815	1 352	2 269	2 465	5	3	0	0	0
Community facilities tax (local)	268	341	446	591	650	705	766	912	1 138	1 351
Tax on excessive land holdings (local)	0	0	0	0	0	0	0	0	0	0
Tax on aggregate land holdings (local)	1 279	1 282	2	0	0	0	0	0	0	0
Rural dev. tax on local agg. land holdings tax	63	81	3	0	0	0	0	0	0	0
Tax on excessively increased land value	-1	0	0	0	0	0	0	0	0	0
Comprehensive real estate tax	0	0	441	1 207	1 029	1 102	1 131	1 224	1 307	1 399
Rural dev. tax on comprehensive real estate tax	0	0	91	242	208	223	228	250	265	267
4110 Households	0	0	0	0	0	0	0	0	0	0
4120 Others	68	138	107	127	101	127	138	156	164	175
Workshop tax on property (local)	68	138	107	127	101	127	138	156	164	175
4200 Recurrent taxes on net wealth	0	0	0	0	0	0	0	0	0	0
4210 Individual	..	..	..	..	..	..	..	..	..	..
4220 Corporate	..	..	..	..	..	..	..	..	..	..
4300 Estate, inheritance and gift taxes	1 161	989	1 873	2 431	3 076	3 333	4 021	4 290	4 625	5 044
4310 Estate and inheritance taxes	605	449	702	1 221	1 203	1 259	1 719	1 587	1 696	1 944
Inheritance tax	605	449	702	1 221	1 203	1 259	1 719	1 587	1 696	1 944
Defence tax on inheritance tax	0	0	0	0	0	0	0	0	0	0
4320 Gift taxes	556	540	1 171	1 210	1 873	2 074	2 302	2 703	2 929	3 100
Gift tax	556	540	1 171	1 210	1 873	2 074	2 302	2 703	2 929	3 100
Defence tax on gift tax	0	0	0	0	0	0	0	0	0	0
4400 Taxes on financial and capital transactions	8 774	11 935	17 796	20 513	21 170	23 443	21 877	20 748	24 026	31 095
Registration tax (local)	4 257	4 528	6 784	7 131	7 370	7 680	7 645	1 312	1 485	1 831
Registration tax	0	0	0	0	0	0	0	0	0	0
Defence tax on registration tax	0	0	0	0	0	0	0	0	0	0
Rural dev. tax on local acquisition tax	164	246	471	621	632	982	853	874	843	969
Rural dev. tax on local registration tax	211	66	64	169	144	2	2	1	1	1
Securities transactions tax	262	2 736	2 370	3 534	3 667	4 279	3 681	3 077	3 121	4 670
Rural dev. tax on securities transaction tax	170	823	958	1 870	2 010	2 515	1 769	1 529	1 459	1 861
Acquisition tax (local)	3 319	3 148	6 649	6 644	6 825	7 361	7 326	13 318	16 391	20 810
Stamp tax	390	388	500	544	522	624	601	637	726	953
4500 Non-recurrent taxes	167	537	-2	0	0	0	0	0	0	0
Asset revaluation tax	167	537	-2	..	..	..	..	..	..	..
4510 On net wealth	..	..	..	..	..	..	..	..	..	..
4520 Other non-recurrent taxes	..	..	..	..	..	..	..	..	..	..
4600 Other recurrent taxes on property	0	0	0	0	0	0	0	0	0	0
5000 Taxes on goods and services	**43 978**	**52 271**	**71 041**	**87 043**	**99 769**	**100 551**	**106 402**	**106 717**	**109 451**	**110 326**
5100 Taxes on production, sale, transfer, etc	41 699	50 023	69 069	84 135	96 573	93 983	99 731	99 970	102 531	103 254
5110 General taxes	19 488	23 212	36 118	46 992	51 800	54 868	58 702	59 105	62 975	60 162
5111 Value added taxes	19 488	23 212	36 118	46 992	51 800	54 868	58 702	59 105	62 975	60 162
Value added tax	19 488	23 212	36 118	46 992	51 800	54 868	58 702	59 105	62 975	60 162
5112 Sales tax	0	0	0	0	0	0	0	0	0	0
Business tax	..	..	..	..	..	..	..	..	..	..
5113 Other	0	0	0	0	0	0	0	0	0	0
5120 Taxes on specific goods and services	22 211	26 811	32 951	37 143	44 773	39 115	41 029	40 865	39 556	43 092

Table 4.4. **Korea** (cont.)

Billion KRW

	1997	2000	2005	2009	2010	2011	2012	2013	2014	2015
5121 Excises	14 616	18 155	24 888	25 341	31 340	25 401	28 410	27 661	28 226	31 857
Commodity tax	0	0	0	0	0	0	0	0	0	0
Defence tax on commodity tax	0	0	0	0	0	0	0	0	0	0
Liquor tax	1 790	1 963	2 601	2 771	2 878	2 529	2 999	2 947	2 852	3 228
Defence tax on liquor tax	0	0	0	0	0	0	0	0	0	0
Education tax on liquor tax	418	516	693	713	724	644	774	764	728	808
Textile tax	0	0	0	0	0	0	0	0	0	0
Petroleum tax	0	0	0	0	0	0	0	0	0	0
Transport tax on petrol products	5 547	8 404	10 288	10 092	13 970	11 546	13 809	13 248	13 440	14 055
Education tax on transport tax	758	1 247	1 543	1 483	2 133	1 726	2 030	1 895	2 074	2 154
Electricity and gas tax	0	0	0	0	0	0	0	0	0	0
Special excise tax	3 036	2 985	4 399	3 642	5 066	5 537	5 336	5 484	5 624	8 001
Defence tax on special excise tax	0	0	0	0	0	0	0	0	0	0
Education tax on special excise tax	804	498	579	322	501	589	525	485	495	515
Rural development on special excise tax	26	37	45	20	24	45	56	56	60	61
Tobacco sales tax (local)	0	0	0	0	0	0	0	0	0	0
Tobacco consumption tax (local)	2 236	2 251	2 448	3 011	2 875	2 785	2 881	2 782	2 953	3 035
Motor fuel tax (local)	0	254	2 292	3 287	3 169	0	0	0	0	0
5122 Profits of fiscal monopolies	0	0	0	0	0	0	0	0	0	0
Monopoly profit	..	..	..	..	..	..	..	..	..	..
5123 Customs and import duties	5 941	5 936	6 530	9 486	11 046	11 350	10 220	11 012	9 132	8 907
Customs duties	5 798	5 800	6 317	9 169	10 666	10 990	9 816	10 562	8 721	8 495
Defence tax on customs duties	0	0	0	0	0	0	0	0	0	0
Special customs duties	0	0	0	0	0	0	0	0	0	0
Tonnage tax	0	0	0	0	0	0	0	0	0	0
Education tax on imports	116	99	173	273	336	322	375	429	390	390
Rural dev. tax on customs exemptions	27	37	40	44	44	38	29	21	21	22
Previous year receipts	0	0	0	0	0	0	0	0	0	0
5124 Taxes on exports	0	0	0	0	0	0	0	0	0	0
5125 Taxes on investment goods	0	0	0	0	0	0	0	0	0	0
5126 Taxes on specific services	1 654	2 720	1 533	2 316	2 387	2 364	2 399	2 192	2 198	2 328
Telephone tax	789	1 457	0	0	0	0	0	0	0	0
Defence tax on telephone tax	0	0	0	0	0	0	0	0	0	0
Entertainment tax	0	0	0	0	0	0	0	0	0	0
Defence tax on entertainment tax	0	0	0	0	0	0	0	0	0	0
Entertainment tax (local)	0	0	0	0	0	0	0	0	0	0
Travel tax	0	0	0	0	0	0	0	0	0	0
Admission tax	0	0	0	0	0	0	0	0	0	0
Defence tax on admission tax	0	0	0	0	0	0	0	0	0	0
Education tax on banking & insurance	369	473	537	964	951	966	932	938	920	1 004
Horse race tax (local)	361	566	692	1 002	1 068	1 072	1 129	1 042	1 073	1 089
Rural dev. tax on horse race tax	18	84	147	203	215	214	221	212	205	235
Butchery tax (local)	47	51	47	56	58	5	0	0	0	0
Regional development tax (local)	71	89	110	91	95	107	117	0	0	0
5127 Other taxes on internat. trade and transactions	0	0	0	0	0	0	0	0	0	0
5128 Other taxes	0	0	0	0	0	0	0	0	0	0
5130 Unallocable between 5110 and 5120	0	0	0	0	0	0	0	0	0	0
5200 Taxes on use of goods and to perform activities	2 279	2 248	1 972	2 908	3 196	6 568	6 671	6 747	6 920	7 072
5210 Recurrent taxes	2 279	2 248	1 972	2 908	3 196	6 568	6 671	6 747	6 920	7 072
Licence tax (local)	225	241	70	74	76	78	78	0	0	0
Automobile tax (local)	2 054	2 007	1 902	2 834	3 120	6 490	6 593	6 747	6 920	7 072
5211 Paid by households: motor vehicles	..	..	..	..	..	..	..	..	..	..
5212 Paid by others: motor vehicles	..	..	..	..	..	..	..	..	..	..
5213 Paid in respect of other goods	..	..	..	..	..	..	..	..	..	..
5220 Non-recurrent taxes	0	0	0	0	0	0	0	0	0	0
5300 Unallocable between 5100 and 5200	0	0	0	0	0	0	0	0	0	0
6000 Other taxes	**4 041**	**4 907**	**6 582**	**12 284**	**9 974**	**9 927**	**11 529**	**10 399**	**10 093**	**9 642**
6100 Paid solely by business	0	0	0	0	0	0	0	0	0	0
6200 Other	4 041	4 907	6 582	12 284	9 974	9 927	11 529	10 399	10 093	9 642
Unallocable tax revenue	0	0	0	0	0	0	0	0	0	0
Previous year tax	779	1 474	2 111	6 890	4 449	4 232	5 768	4 774	4 049	3 435
Previous year tax (local)	340	474	633	600	654	728	680	601	589	392
Unallocable defence tax	-8	-3	-9	0	0	0	0	0	0	0
Education tax on local taxes	2 931	2 962	3 847	4 794	4 871	4 967	5 081	5 024	5 455	5 815

Table 4.4. **Korea** (cont.)

Note:

Figures are taken from OECD (2016), *Revenue Statistics 2016*, *http://dx.doi.org/10.1787/rev_stats-2016-en-fr*, and are preliminary for 2015.
Year ending 31st December.

Data are on a cash basis.

Heading 2000: From 1997 the contributions to the three funds (civil servant pension fund, private school teachers' pension fund and medical insurance fund) are classified as security social contributions. The reasons for the change are that the contributions either became mandatory or the fund started to be managed by public authorities in that year, thereby meeting the OECD definition of social security contributions.

Heading 2200: From 2007, this includes long-term care insurance.

Source: Ministry of Finance and Economy, Ministry of Home Affairs.

StatLink ᴍᴤᴘ *http://dx.doi.org/10.1787/888933544322*

Table 4.5. **Malaysia**

Million MYR

	1997	2000	2005	2009	2010	2011	2012	2013	2014	2015
Total tax revenue	**56 905**	**51 857**	**87 563**	**114 754**	**118 302**	**144 297**	**161 539**	**166 269**	**175 452**	**177 323**
1000 Taxes on income, profits and capital gains	**27 648**	**27 339**	**51 040**	**75 269**	**75 058**	**98 018**	**111 676**	**114 113**	**120 284**	**105 751**
1100 Of individuals	6 429	7 015	8 649	15 590	17 805	20 203	22 977	23 055	24 423	26 321
1110 On income and profits	6 429	7 015	8 649	15 590	17 805	20 203	22 977	23 055	24 423	26 321
1120 On capital gains	..	..	..	..	..	..	..	..	..	..
1200 Corporate	20 552	19 923	40 962	57 725	55 156	74 653	85 239	87 949	92 223	75 275
1210 On profits	20 552	19 923	40 962	57 725	55 156	74 653	85 239	87 949	92 223	75 275
Company income tax	16 688	13 905	26 381	30 199	36 266	46 888	51 288	58 175	65 240	63 679
Petroleum income tax	3 861	6 010	14 566	27 231	18 713	27 748	33 934	29 753	26 956	11 559
Offshore business activity tax	3	8	15	15	15	17	18	20	27	37
Levy on electricity	0	0	0	280	162	0	0	1	0	0
1220 On capital gains	..	..	..	..	..	..	..	..	..	..
1300 Unallocable between 1100 and 1200	666	402	1 429	1 954	2 097	3 162	3 459	3 109	3 639	4 155
Cooperatives income tax	143	87	63	546	378	357	345	286	169	80
Withholding income tax	0	0	1 110	1 328	1 268	1 519	2 097	2 008	2 184	2 316
Other income tax	0	0	20	23	21	17	21	23	24	30
Real property gains tax	523	247	236	42	303	509	608	785	1 210	1 729
Exit levy	0	41	0	0	0	0	0	0	0	0
Windfall levy on crude palm oil	0	0	0	0	0	0	0	0	0	0
Windfall levy on crude palm kernel oil	0	26	0	0	0	0	0	0	0	0
Levy on fresh fruit bunch	0	0	0	16	127	761	388	7	51	1
2000 Social security contributions	**0**	**990**	**1 382**	**1 867**	**2 008**	**2 172**	**2 326**	**2 518**	**2 689**	**2 900**
2100 Employees	..	218	304	409	439	475	508	552	588	..
2110 On a payroll basis	..	218	304	409	439	475	508	552	588	..
2120 On an income tax basis	..	0	0	0	0	0	0	0	0	..
2200 Employers	..	772	1 079	1 458	1 569	1 697	1 818	1 966	2 101	..
2210 On a payroll basis	..	772	1 079	1 458	1 569	1 697	1 818	1 966	2 101	..
2220 On an income tax basis	..	0	0	0	0	0	0	0	0	..
2300 Self-employed or non-employed	..	0	0	0	0	0	0	0	0	..
2310 On a payroll basis	..	..	..	..	..	..	..	..	..	..
2320 On an income tax basis	..	..	..	..	..	..	..	..	..	..
2400 Unallocable between 2100, 2200 and 2300	..	0	0	0	0	0	0	0	0	2 900
2410 On a payroll basis	..	..	..	..	..	..	..	..	..	..
2420 On an income tax basis	..	..	..	..	..	..	..	..	..	..
3000 Taxes on payroll and workforce	**0**	**0**	**0**	**0**	**0**	**0**	**0**	**0**	**0**	**0**
4000 Taxes on property	**1 431**	**1 776**	**3 427**	**4 471**	**4 729**	**5 009**	**5 243**	**5 350**	**5 941**	**6 300**
4100 Recurrent taxes on immovable property	1 412	1 774	3 422	4 471	4 729	5 009	5 241	5 349	5 939	6 299
Quit rent	..	..	942	1 284	1 385	1 501	1 561	1 489	1 549	1 799
4110 Households	1 412	1 774	2 480	3 187	3 344	3 508	3 680	3 860	4 390	4 500
Assessment tax	1 412	1 774	2 480	3 187	3 344	3 508	3 680	3 860	4 390	4 500
4120 Others	0	0	0	0	0	0	0	0	0	0
4200 Recurrent taxes on net wealth	0	0	0	0	0	0	0	0	0	0
4210 Individual	..	..	..	..	..	..	..	..	..	..
4220 Corporate	..	..	..	..	..	..	..	..	..	..
4300 Estate, inheritance and gift taxes	19	2	5	0	0	0	2	1	2	1
4310 Estate and inheritance taxes	19	2	5	..	..	..	2	1	2	1
Estate duty	19	2	5	..	..	..	2	1	2	1
4320 Gift taxes	0	0	0	..	..	..	0	0	0	0
4400 Taxes on financial and capital transactions	0	0	0	0	0	0	0	0	0	0
4500 Non-recurrent taxes	0	0	0	0	0	0	0	0	0	0
4510 On net wealth	..	..	..	..	..	..	..	..	..	..
4520 Other non-recurrent taxes	..	..	..	..	..	..	..	..	..	..
4600 Other recurrent taxes on property	0	0	0	0	0	0	0	0	0	0
5000 Taxes on goods and services	**25 061**	**19 910**	**29 216**	**29 746**	**32 268**	**34 114**	**36 647**	**37 871**	**40 030**	**56 353**
5100 Taxes on production, sale, transfer, etc	23 195	17 990	27 051	27 834	30 218	31 883	34 317	35 421	37 411	53 669
5110 General taxes	6 167	5 968	7 709	8 603	8 171	8 577	9 496	10 068	10 939	32 235
5111 Value added taxes	0	0	0	0	0	0	0	0	0	27 012
5112 Sales tax	6 167	5 968	7 709	8 603	8 171	8 577	9 496	10 068	10 939	5 223
On local goods	4 160	3 894	5 403	5 348	4 886	4 995	5 358	5 626	6 130	3 207
On imported goods	2 008	2 074	2 306	3 255	3 285	3 583	4 138	4 442	4 809	2 016
5113 Other	0	0	0	0	0	0	0	0	0	0
5120 Taxes on specific goods and services	15 266	10 245	17 511	16 822	19 624	20 765	22 184	22 756	23 930	18 862

Table 4.5. **Malaysia** (cont.)

Million MYR

	1997	2000	2005	2009	2010	2011	2012	2013	2014	2015
5121 Excise duties	6 053	3 803	9 322	10 068	11 770	11 517	12 187	12 193	12 925	11 890
On local goods	6 053	3 803	8 641	8 474	9 350	8 415	8 420	8 395	8 456	7 999
On imported goods	0	0	680	1 595	2 420	3 102	3 767	3 798	4 468	3 891
5122 Profits of fiscal monopolies	0	0	0	0	0	0	0	0	0	0
5123 Customs and import duties	6 524	3 599	3 385	2 114	1 966	2 026	2 282	2 524	2 670	2 732
5124 Taxes on exports	1 053	1 032	2 085	1 152	1 810	2 081	1 968	1 930	1 893	1 039
5125 Taxes on investment goods	0	0	0	0	0	0	0	0	0	0
5126 Taxes on specific services	1 475	1 701	2 582	3 344	3 926	4 982	5 583	5 944	6 278	3 038
Pool betting duties and sweepstakes	0	0	0	0	0	0	0	0	0	0
Service tax	1 475	1 701	2 582	3 344	3 926	4 982	5 583	5 944	6 278	3 038
5127 Other taxes on internat. trade and transactions	160	110	137	143	151	159	164	165	165	163
5128 Other taxes	0	0	0	0	0	0	0	0	0	0
5130 Unallocable between 5110 and 5120	1 761	1 777	1 831	2 409	2 423	2 541	2 638	2 597	2 542	2 572
5200 Taxes on use of goods and to perform activities	1 866	1 920	2 165	1 912	2 050	2 231	2 329	2 450	2 619	2 684
5210 Recurrent taxes	1 863	1 918	2 163	1 909	2 047	2 227	2 326	2 447	2 617	2 681
5211 Paid by households: motor vehicles	1 852	1 909	2 147	1 856	1 992	2 183	2 283	2 407	2 532	2 630
Motor vehicle licences	1 852	1 909	2 147	1 856	1 992	2 183	2 283	2 407	2 532	2 630
5212 Paid by others: motor vehicles	11	9	15	17	18	5	3	3	3	3
Commercial vehicle licences	11	9	14	16	17	5	3	3	3	3
Tour vehicle licences	0	0	1	1	1	1	0	0	0	0
5213 Paid in respect of other goods	0	0	1	36	38	39	39	37	81	48
Petroleum permits	0	0	1	1	1	1	1	0	4	2
Bank licences fees	0	0	0	35	37	38	39	37	78	46
5220 Non-recurrent taxes	3	2	2	2	2	4	3	2	2	3
Environment pollution licences	2	2	2	2	2	4	3	2	2	3
Film rental tax	1	0	0	0	0	0	0	0	0	0
5300 Unallocable between 5100 and 5200	0	0	0	0	0	0	0	0	0	0
6000 Other taxes	**2 764**	**1 841**	**2 499**	**3 401**	**4 240**	**4 984**	**5 648**	**6 417**	**6 508**	**6 018**
6100 Paid solely by business	0	0	0	0	0	0	0	0	0	0
6200 Other	2 764	1 841	2 499	3 401	4 240	4 984	5 648	6 417	6 508	6 018
Share transfer tax	0	0	0	0	0	0	0	0	0	0
Stamp duties	2 714	1 799	2 460	3 349	4 192	4 929	5 595	6 364	6 458	5 974
Other direct taxes	50	42	38	52	48	55	53	53	51	45

Note:

Year ending 31st December.

The data are on a cash basis.

Heading 2000: The data are estimated for 2015. An average annual growth rate for the period 2012-2014 was applied to the 2014 figure.

Heading 4100: The data for the quit rent and the assessment tax are estimated for 2015.

Heading 5111: The data for 2015 are sourced from the IMF's Government Finance Statistics dataset.

Source: Ministry of Finance of Malaysia, Social Security Organisation, State Government Financial Report and Local Government Financial Report.

StatLink ᴴᴵᴸ *http://dx.doi.org/10.1787/888933544341*

Table 4.6. **Philippines**

Million PHP

	1997	2000	2005	2009	2010	2011	2012	2013	2014	2015
Total tax revenue	**447 976**	**564 343**	**863 599**	**1 205 348**	**1 330 768**	**1 469 547**	**1 669 306**	**1 868 601**	**2 111 568**	**2 262 150**
1000 Taxes on income, profits and capital gains	**164 170**	**217 798**	**344 954**	**467 706**	**521 707**	**612 432**	**691 232**	**767 819**	**840 680**	**912 198**
1100 Of individuals	59 749	83 006	118 582	137 108	167 605	194 025	223 165	246 894	283 873	309 439
1110 On income and profits	53 370	78 229	113 549	130 074	158 325	184 076	210 645	232 725	267 703	292 548
1120 On capital gains	6 379	4 777	5 033	7 033	9 280	9 949	12 520	14 169	16 170	16 891
1200 Corporate	95 449	116 980	190 628	303 391	326 967	392 400	432 850	486 898	523 183	569 454
1210 On profits	94 427	114 871	188 876	297 900	323 116	387 499	421 937	476 311	513 978	561 434
1220 On capital gains	1 022	2 110	1 752	5 492	3 851	4 902	10 913	10 587	9 205	8 020
1300 Unallocable between 1100 and 1200	8 973	17 812	35 744	27 207	27 135	26 007	35 217	34 027	33 624	33 305
2000 Social security contributions	**36 500**	**74 200**	**107 900**	**156 000**	**168 430**	**186 203**	**215 356**	**236 575**	**284 360**	**316 142**
2100 Employees	..	..	..	..	..	..	..	..	..	..
2110 On a payroll basis	..	..	..	..	..	..	..	..	..	..
2120 On an income tax basis	..	..	..	..	..	..	..	..	..	..
2200 Employers	2 800	19 900	23 300	33 000	34 300	38 008	54 215	54 662	80 130	94 663
2210 On a payroll basis	..	..	..	..	..	..	..	..	..	..
2220 On an income tax basis	..	..	..	..	..	..	..	..	..	..
2300 Self-employed or non-employed	..	..	..	..	..	..	..	..	..	..
2310 On a payroll basis	..	..	..	..	..	..	..	..	..	..
2320 On an income tax basis	..	..	..	..	..	..	..	..	..	..
2400 Unallocable between 2100, 2200 and 2300	33 700	54 300	84 600	123 000	134 130	148 195	161 141	181 913	204 230	221 479
2410 On a payroll basis	..	..	..	..	..	..	..	..	..	..
2420 On an income tax basis	..	..	..	..	..	..	..	..	..	..
3000 Taxes on payroll and workforce	**0**	**0**	**0**	**0**	**0**	**0**	**0**	**0**	**0**	**0**
4000 Taxes on property	**4 178**	**17 401**	**29 463**	**36 963**	**39 070**	**44 590**	**50 943**	**56 269**	**60 026**	**63 990**
4100 Recurrent taxes on immovable property	0	14 947	25 697	31 518	31 876	36 043	39 315	41 191	45 458	48 999
Real property tax (local government)	..	14 947	25 697	31 518	31 876	36 043	39 315	41 191	45 458	48 999
4110 Households	..	..	..	..	..	..	..	..	..	..
4120 Others	..	..	..	..	..	..	..	..	..	..
4200 Recurrent taxes on net wealth	0	0	0	0	0	0	0	0	0	0
4210 Individual	..	..	..	..	..	..	..	..	..	..
4220 Corporate	..	..	..	..	..	..	..	..	..	..
4300 Estate, inheritance and gift taxes	881	480	1 017	1 426	1 981	2 400	3 626	3 275	5 450	5 636
4310 Estate and inheritance taxes	677	302	693	982	1 451	1 635	2 315	1 650	3 489	3 341
4320 Gift taxes	204	178	324	444	531	765	1 312	1 625	1 960	2 294
4400 Taxes on financial and capital transactions	3 297	1 974	2 749	4 019	5 213	6 147	8 002	11 803	9 118	9 356
Stock transactions (RA 7717)	3 297	1 974	2 749	4 019	5 213	6 147	8 002	11 803	9 118	9 356
4500 Non-recurrent taxes	0	0	0	0	0	0	0	0	0	0
4510 On net wealth	..	..	..	..	..	..	..	..	..	..
4520 Other non-recurrent taxes	..	..	..	..	..	..	..	..	..	..
4600 Other recurrent taxes on property	0	0	0	0	0	0	0	0	0	0
5000 Taxes on goods and services	**225 025**	**237 243**	**344 362**	**498 883**	**549 890**	**568 870**	**648 504**	**735 896**	**844 442**	**884 132**
5100 Taxes on production, sale, transfer, etc	222 627	234 202	337 155	489 850	540 595	558 770	638 148	724 888	832 656	872 832
5110 General taxes	47 273	53 879	87 855	168 294	173 284	183 082	229 594	250 149	278 794	295 502
5111 Value added taxes	47 273	53 879	87 855	168 294	173 284	183 082	229 594	250 149	278 794	295 502
5112 Sales tax	0	0	0	0	0	0	0	0	0	0
5113 Other	0	0	0	0	0	0	0	0	0	0
5120 Taxes on specific goods and services	175 354	180 323	249 300	321 556	367 312	375 687	408 554	474 739	553 862	577 330
5121 Excises	63 048	61 677	61 816	60 548	67 203	67 993	72 346	118 856	135 315	158 319
Alcohol products	13 412	12 997	17 012	20 637	21 781	22 873	23 896	33 535	37 525	42 214
Tobacco products	16 027	17 427	23 709	24 236	31 730	25 997	32 942	71 608	82 725	99 505
Petroleum products	29 272	28 297	18 709	12 772	9 832	9 963	10 159	8 503	9 419	11 888
Automobiles	0	0	0	0	0	2 026	2 935	2 542	2 636	2 452
Mineral products	77	243	251	719	1 306	6 986	2 206	2 494	2 814	2 079
Others	4 259	2 712	2 134	2 183	2 555	148	208	174	196	182
5122 Profits of fiscal monopolies	0	0	0	0	0	0	0	0	0	0
5123 Customs and import duties	94 800	95 006	154 566	220 307	259 241	265 108	289 866	304 925	369 277	367 534
5124 Taxes on exports	0	0	0	0	0	0	0	0	0	0
5125 Taxes on investment goods	0	0	0	0	0	0	0	0	0	0
5126 Taxes on specific services	17 506	23 639	32 919	40 701	40 868	42 587	46 342	50 958	49 270	51 477
Banks and financial institutions	9 696	9 538	14 892	21 937	22 857	23 514	25 338	30 199	26 677	26 915
Travel tax (CHED/NCAA)	386	1 043	1 164	1 843	1 512	1 660	1 709	1 885	1 827	1 770
Immigration tax (BID)	18	47	40	39	59	61	64	69	72	72
Others	7 406	13 011	16 823	16 882	16 440	17 351	19 231	18 805	20 694	22 720
5127 Other taxes on internat. trade and transactions	0	0	0	0	0	0	0	0	0	0

Table 4.6. **Philippines** (cont.)

Million PHP

	1997	2000	2005	2009	2010	2011	2012	2013	2014	2015
5128 Other taxes	0	0	0	0	0	0	0	0	0	0
5130 Unallocable between 5110 and 5120	0	0	0	0	0	0	0	0	0	0
5200 Taxes on use of goods and perform activities	2 398	3 041	7 207	9 033	9 295	10 100	10 356	11 008	11 786	11 300
5210 Recurrent taxes	2 398	3 041	7 207	9 033	9 295	10 100	10 356	11 008	11 786	11 300
LTO-Motor vehicle users' tax	2 398	3 041	7 207	9 033	9 295	10 100	10 356	11 008	11 786	11 300
5211 Paid by households: motor vehicles	..	..	..	..	..	..	..	..	..	..
5212 Paid by others: motor vehicles	..	..	..	..	..	..	..	..	..	..
5213 Paid in respect of other goods	0	0	0	0	0	0	0	0	0	0
5220 Non-recurrent taxes	0	0	0	0	0	0	0	0	0	0
5300 Unallocable between 5100 and 5200	0	0	0	0	0	0	0	0	0	0
6000 Other taxes	**18 103**	**17 702**	**36 921**	**45 797**	**51 671**	**57 452**	**63 271**	**72 042**	**82 060**	**85 687**
6100 Paid solely by business	0	0	0	0	0	0	0	0	0	0
6200 Other	18 103	17 702	36 921	45 797	51 671	57 452	63 271	72 042	82 060	85 687
Documentary stamp tax	16 477	16 170	29 431	37 484	42 629	47 879	52 455	60 356	69 036	72 073
DENR-Forest charges	116	175	84	132	239	150	204	132	133	128
Miscellaneous taxes	1 510	1 356	4 543	4 317	4 391	4 724	5 788	5 874	6 051	6 219
Other taxes (local government)	0	0	2 863	3 864	4 412	4 700	4 823	5 679	6 840	7 267

Note:

Year ending 31st December.

The data are on a cash basis.

Heading 5123: This category includes VAT and excises levied on imports.

Source: Department of Finance of the Philippines.

StatLink ⌐≡ *http://dx.doi.org/10.1787/888933544360*

Table 4.7. **Singapore**

Details of tax revenue

Million SGD

	1997	2000	2005	2009	2010	2011	2012	2013	2014	2015
Total tax revenue	..	**25 627**	**25 687**	**36 616**	**41 848**	**46 076**	**50 119**	**51 146**	**54 110**	**55 647**
1000 Taxes on income, profits and capital gains	..	**13 538**	**12 912**	**17 211**	**18 687**	**20 579**	**22 411**	**22 050**	**23 940**	**24 890**
1100 Of individuals	..	3 543	3 425	6 114	6 470	6 871	7 714	7 688	8 927	9 235
1110 On income and profits	..	3 543	3 425	6 114	6 470	6 871	7 714	7 688	8 927	9 235
1120 On capital gains	..	0	0	0	0	0	0	0	0	0
1200 Corporate	..	9 509	8 589	9 961	11 260	12 450	13 360	13 209	13 887	14 253
1210 On profits	..	9 509	8 589	9 961	11 260	12 450	13 360	13 209	13 887	14 253
From corporate profits	..	8 316	7 340	9 551	10 687	12 096	12 821	12 680	13 372	13 815
Statutory board contributions	..	1 192	1 249	410	573	353	539	530	516	438
1220 On capital gains	..	0	0	0	0	0	0	0	0	0
1300 Unallocable between 1100 and 1200	..	486	898	1 137	957	1 258	1 337	1 152	1 126	1 402
Withholding taxes	..	486	898	1 137	957	1 258	1 337	1 152	1 126	1 402
2000 Social security contributions	..	**0**	**0**	**0**	**0**	**0**	**0**	**0**	**0**	**0**
2100 Employees	..	..	..	..	..	..	..	..	..	..
2110 On a payroll basis	..	..	..	..	..	..	..	..	..	..
2120 On an income tax basis	..	..	..	..	..	..	..	..	..	..
2200 Employers	..	..	..	..	..	..	..	..	..	..
2210 On a payroll basis	..	..	..	..	..	..	..	..	..	..
2220 On an income tax basis	..	..	..	..	..	..	..	..	..	..
2300 Self-employed or non-employed	..	..	..	..	..	..	..	..	..	..
2310 On a payroll basis	..	..	..	..	..	..	..	..	..	..
2320 On an income tax basis	..	..	..	..	..	..	..	..	..	..
2400 Unallocable between 2100, 2200 and 2300	..	..	..	..	..	..	..	..	..	..
2410 On a payroll basis	..	..	..	..	..	..	..	..	..	..
2420 On an income tax basis	..	..	..	..	..	..	..	..	..	..
3000 Taxes on payroll and workforce	..	**0**	**0**	**0**	**0**	**0**	**0**	**0**	**0**	**0**
4000 Taxes on property	..	**2 863**	**2 876**	**4 374**	**6 080**	**7 077**	**8 078**	**8 112**	**7 124**	**7 224**
4100 Recurrent taxes on immovable property	..	1 535	1 829	1 979	2 798	3 899	3 760	4 179	4 340	4 456
4110 Households	..	..	..	..	..	..	..	..	..	..
4120 Others	..	..	..	..	..	..	..	..	..	..
4200 Recurrent taxes on net wealth	..	0	0	0	0	0	0	0	0	0
4210 Individual	..	..	..	..	..	..	..	..	..	..
4220 Corporate	..	..	..	..	..	..	..	..	..	..
4300 Estate, inheritance and gift taxes	..	71	81	8	5	3	8	3	1	-1
4310 Estate and inheritance taxes	..	71	81	8	5	3	8	3	1	-1
4320 Gift taxes	..	0	0	0	0	0	0	0	0	0
4400 Taxes on financial and capital transactions	..	1 257	967	2 386	3 277	3 175	4 310	3 930	2 784	2 769
4500 Non-recurrent taxes	..	0	0	0	0	0	0	0	0	0
4510 On net wealth	..	..	..	..	..	..	..	..	..	..
4520 Other non-recurrent taxes	..	..	..	..	..	..	..	..	..	..
4600 Other recurrent taxes on property	..	0	0	0	0	0	0	0	0	0
5000 Taxes on goods and services	..	**7 967**	**8 722**	**12 622**	**14 376**	**15 113**	**15 288**	**15 736**	**16 949**	**17 657**
5100 Taxes on production, sale, transfer, etc	..	5 462	7 289	10 766	12 525	13 193	13 485	14 081	15 346	15 897
5110 General taxes	..	2 121	3 815	6 914	8 198	8 687	9 038	9 513	10 215	10 345
5111 Value added taxes	..	2 121	3 815	6 914	8 198	8 687	9 038	9 513	10 215	10 345
5112 Sales tax	..	0	0	0	0	0	0	0	0	0
5113 Other	..	0	0	0	0	0	0	0	0	0
5120 Taxes on specific goods and services	..	3 341	3 474	3 852	4 327	4 506	4 447	4 568	5 131	5 552
5121 Excises	..	1 847	1 974	2 125	2 048	2 133	2 142	2 189	2 540	2 833
Liquors	..	..	368	433	470	496	517	518	634	638
Tobacco	..	..	713	932	889	967	969	1 043	1 228	1 205
Petroleum Products	..	..	373	413	419	416	415	414	419	584
Motor Vehicles	..	..	518	344	267	248	233	206	251	399
Compressed Natural Gas Unit Duty	..	..	0	0	0	1	3	3	3	2
Others	..	..	3	4	5	5	5	5	6	5
5122 Profits of fiscal monopolies	..	0	0	0	0	0	0	0	0	0
5123 Customs and import duties	..	..	..	..	..	..	..	..	..	..
5124 Taxes on exports	..	0	0	0	0	0	0	0	0	0
5125 Taxes on investment goods	..	0	0	0	0	0	0	0	0	0
5126 Taxes on specific services	..	1 494	1 501	1 727	2 279	2 373	2 305	2 379	2 591	2 719
Betting duty	..	1 494	1 501	1 727	2 279	2 373	2 305	2 379	2 591	2 719
5127 Other taxes on internat. trade and transactions	..	0	0	0	0	0	0	0	0	0
5128 Other taxes	..	0	0	0	0	0	0	0	0	0
5130 Unallocable between 5110 and 5120	..	0	0	0	0	0	0	0	0	0

Table 4.7. **Singapore** (cont.)
Details of tax revenue

Million SGD

	1997	2000	2005	2009	2010	2011	2012	2013	2014	2015
5200 Taxes on use of goods and perform activities	..	2 506	1 432	1 856	1 851	1 920	1 803	1 655	1 603	1 760
5210 Recurrent taxes	..	..	..	..	..	..	..	..	..	..
5211 Paid by households: motor vehicles	..	..	..	..	..	..	..	..	..	..
5212 Paid by others: motor vehicles	..	..	..	..	..	..	..	..	..	..
5213 Paid in respect of other goods	..	..	..	..	..	..	..	..	..	..
5220 Non-recurrent taxes	..	..	..	..	..	..	..	..	..	..
5300 Unallocable between 5100 and 5200	..	0	0	0	0	0	0	0	0	0
6000 Other taxes	..	**1 259**	**1 177**	**2 410**	**2 706**	**3 307**	**4 342**	**5 248**	**6 097**	**5 876**
6100 Paid solely by business	..	0	0	0	0	0	0	0	0	0
6200 Other	..	1 259	1 177	2 410	2 706	3 307	4 342	5 248	6 097	5 876

Note:

Data are on a fiscal year basis ending 31st March. For example, the data for 2014 represent 1 April 2014 to 31 March 2015. The data are on a cash basis.

Heading 2000: There are no social security contributions in Singapore.

Heading 4100: Recurrent taxes on immovable property includes tax levied on all private properties, as well as properties owned by statutory boards.

Heading 5121: Comprises excises, customs and import duties.

Source: Ministry of Finance of Singapore.

StatLink *http://dx.doi.org/10.1787/888933544379*

ANNEX A

The OECD Interpretative Guide[1]

Table of contents

		Page
A.1.	The OECD classification of taxes	78
A.2.	Coverage	80
A.3.	Basis of reporting	82
A.4.	General classification criteria	83
A.5.	Commentaries on items of the list	85
A.6.	Conciliation with National Accounts	95
A.7.	Memorandum item on the financing of social security benefits	95
A.8.	Memorandum item on identifiable taxes paid by government	95
A.9.	Relation of OECD classification of taxes to national accounting systems	95
A.10.	Relation of OECD classification of taxes to the International Monetary Fund system	96
A.11.	Comparison of the OECD classification of taxes with other international classifications	96
A.12.	Attribution of tax revenues by subsectors of general government	98
A.13.	Provisional classification of revenues from bank levies and payments to deposit insurance and financial stability schemes	100
Notes		102

A.1. The OECD classification of taxes

1000   *Taxes on income, profits and capital gains*

     1100 Taxes on income, profits and capital gains of individuals

         1110 On income and profits

         1120 On capital gains

     1200 Corporate taxes on income, profits and capital gains

         1210 On income and profits

         1220 On capital gains

     1300 Unallocable as between 1100 and 1200

2000   *Social security contributions*

     2100 Employees

         2110 On a payroll basis

         2120 On an income tax basis

     2200 Employers

         2210 On a payroll basis

         2220 On an income tax basis

     2300 Self-employed, non-employed

         2310 On a payroll basis

         2320 On an income tax basis

     2400 Unallocable as between 2100, 2200 and 2300

         2410 On a payroll basis

         2420 On an income tax basis

3000   *Taxes on payroll and workforce*

4000   *Taxes on property*

     4100 Recurrent taxes on immovable property

         4110 Households

         4120 Other

     4200 Recurrent taxes on net wealth

         4210 Individual

         4220 Corporate

     4300 Estate, inheritance and gift taxes

         4310 Estate and inheritance taxes

         4320 Gift taxes

     4400 Taxes on financial and capital transactions

4500 Other non-recurrent taxes on property

    4510 On net wealth

    4520 Other non-recurrent taxes

4600 Other recurrent taxes on property

5000   *Taxes on goods and services*

5100 Taxes on production, sale, transfer, leasing and delivery of goods and rendering of services

    5110 General taxes

        5111 Value-added taxes

        5112 Sales taxes

        5113 Other general taxes on goods and services

    5120 Taxes on specific goods and services

        5121 Excises

        5122 Profits of fiscal monopolies

        5123 Customs and import duties

        5124 Taxes on exports

        5125 Taxes on investment goods

        5126 Taxes on specific services

        5127 Other taxes on international trade and transactions

        5128 Other taxes on specific goods and services

    5130 Unallocable as between 5110 and 5120

5200 Taxes on use of goods, or on permission to use goods or perform activities

    5210 Recurrent taxes

        5211 Paid by households in respect of motor vehicles

        5212 Paid by others in respect of motor vehicles

        5213 Other recurrent taxes

    5220 Non-recurrent taxes

5300 Unallocable as between 5100 and 5200

6000   *Other taxes*

6100 Paid solely by business

6200 Paid by other than business, or unidentifiable

The OECD Interpretative Guide[1]

A.2. Coverage

General criteria

1.   In the OECD classification the term "taxes" is confined to compulsory unrequited payments to general government. Taxes are unrequited in the sense that benefits provided by government to taxpayers are not normally in proportion to their payments.

2.   The term 'tax' does not include fines, penalties and compulsory loans paid to government. Borderline cases between tax and non-tax revenues in relation to certain fees and charges are discussed in §9–12.

3.   General government consists of the central administration, agencies whose operations are under its effective control, state and local governments and their administrations, certain social security schemes and autonomous governmental entities, excluding public enterprises. This definition of government follows that of the 2008 System of National Accounts (SNA).[2] In that publication, the general government sector and its sub-sectors are defined in chapter 4, section F, pages 80-84.

4.   Compulsory payments to supra-national bodies and their agencies are no longer included as taxes as from 1998, with some exceptions. However, custom duties collected by EU member states on behalf of the European Union are still identified as memorandum items and included in overall tax revenue amounts in the country tables (Chapter 4) of the country in which they are collected. (See §94). In countries where the church forms part of general government church taxes are included, provided they meet the criteria set out in §1 above. As the data refer to receipts of general government, levies paid to non-government bodies, welfare agencies or social insurance schemes outside general government, trade unions or trade associations, even where such levies are compulsory, are excluded. Compulsory payments to general government earmarked for such bodies are, however, included, provided that the government is not simply acting in an agency capacity.[3] Profits from fiscal monopolies are distinguished from those of other public enterprises and are treated as taxes because they reflect the exercise of the taxing power of the state by the use of monopoly powers (see §61–63), as are profits received by the government from the purchase and sale of foreign exchange at different rates (see §69).

5.   Taxes paid by governments (e.g., social security contributions and payroll taxes paid by governments in their capacity as an employer, consumption taxes on their purchases or taxes on their property) are not excluded from the data provided. However, where it is possible to identify the amounts of revenue involved,[4] they are shown in Chapter 4.3 of this Report.

6.   The relationship between this classification and that of the System of National Accounts (SNA) is set out in Sections A.9 and A.11 below. Because of the differences between the two classifications, the data shown in national accounts are sometimes calculated or classified differently from the practice set out in this guide. These and other differences are mentioned where appropriate (e.g., in §25 below) but it is not possible to refer to all of them. There may also be some differences between this classification and that employed domestically by certain national administrations (e.g., see §10 below), so that OECD and national statistics data may not always be consistent: any such differences, however, are likely to be very slight in terms of amounts of revenues involved.

Social security contributions

7.   Compulsory social security contributions, as defined in §34 below, paid to general government, are treated here as tax revenues. Being compulsory payments to general government they clearly resemble taxes. They may, however, differ from other taxes in that the receipt of social security benefits depends, in most countries, upon appropriate contributions having been made, although the size of the benefits is not necessarily related to the amount of the contributions. Better comparability between countries is obtained by treating social security contributions as taxes, but they are listed under a separate heading so that they can be distinguished in any analysis.

8.   Social security contributions which are either voluntary or not payable to general government (see §1) are not treated as taxes, though in some countries, as indicated in the country footnotes, there are difficulties in eliminating voluntary contributions and certain compulsory payments to the private sector. Imputed social security contributions are also not treated as taxes.

Fees, user charges and licence fees

9.   Apart from vehicle licence fees, which are universally regarded as taxes, it is not easy to distinguish between those fees and user charges which are to be treated as taxes and those which are not, since, whilst a fee or charge is levied in connection with a specific service or activity, the strength of the link between the fee and the service provided may vary considerably, as may the relation between the amount of the fee and the cost of providing the service. Where the recipient of a service pays a fee clearly related to the cost of providing the service, the levy may be regarded as requited and under the definition of §1 would not be considered as a tax. In the following cases, however, a levy could be considered as 'unrequited':

    a)   where the charge greatly exceeds the cost of providing the service;

    b)   where the payer of the levy is not the receiver of the benefit (e.g. a fee collected from slaughterhouses to finance a service which is provided to farmers);

    c)   where government is not providing a specific service in return for the levy which it receives even though a licence may be issued to the payer (e.g. where the government grants a hunting, fishing or shooting licence which is not accompanied by the right to use a specific area of government land);

    d)   where benefits are received only by those paying the levy but the benefits received by each individual are not necessarily in proportion to his payments (e.g. a milk marketing levy paid by dairy farmers and used to promote the consumption of milk).

10. In marginal cases, however, the application of the criteria set out in §1 can be particularly difficult. The solution adopted – given the desirability of international uniformity and the relatively small amounts of revenue usually involved – is to follow the predominant practice among tax administrations rather than to allow each country to adopt its own view as to whether such levies are regarded as taxes or as non-tax revenue.[5]

11. A list of the main fees and charges in question and their normal[6] treatment in this publication is as follows:

Non-tax revenues: court fees; driving licence fees; harbour fees; passport fees; radio and television licence fees where public authorities provide the service.

<table>
<tr><td>Taxes within
heading 5200:</td><td>permission to perform such activities as distributing films; hunting, fishing and shooting; providing entertainment or gambling facilities; selling alcohol or tobacco; permission to own dogs or to use or own motor vehicles or guns; severance taxes.</td></tr>
</table>

12. In practice it may not always be possible to isolate tax receipts from non-tax revenue receipts when they are recorded together. If it is estimated that the bulk of the receipts derive from non-tax revenues, the whole amount involved is treated as a non-tax revenue; otherwise, such government receipts are included and classified according to the rules provided in §27 below.

Royalties

13. Royalty payments for the right to extract oil and gas or to exploit other mineral resources are normally regarded as non-tax revenues since they are property income from government-owned land or resources.

Fines and penalties

14. In principle, fines and penalties charged on overdue taxes or penalties imposed for the attempted evasion of taxes should not be recorded as tax revenues. However it may not be possible to separate payments of fines or other penalties from the revenues from the taxes to which they relate. In this case the fines and penalties relating to a particular tax are recorded together with the revenues from that tax and fines and penalties paid with revenue from unidentifiable taxes are classified as other taxes in Category 6000. Fines not relating to tax offences (e.g. for parking offences), or not identifiable as relating to tax offences, are also not treated as tax revenues.

A.3. Basis of reporting

Accrual reporting

15. The data reported in this publication for recent years are predominantly recorded on an accrual basis, i.e. recorded at the time that the tax liability was created. Further information is provided in the footnotes to the country table in Chapter 4 of the Report.

16. However, data for earlier years are still predominantly recorded on a cash basis, i.e. at the time at which the payment was received by government. Thus, for example, taxes withheld by employers in one year but paid to the government in the following year and taxes due in one year but actually paid in the following year are both included in the receipts of the second year. Corrective transactions, such as refunds, repayments and drawbacks, are deducted from gross revenues of the period in which they are made.

17. Data on tax revenues are recorded without offsets for the administrative expenses connected with tax collection. Similarly, where the proceeds of tax are used to subsidise particular members of the community, the subsidy is not deducted from the yield of the tax, though the tax may be shown net of subsidies in the national records of some countries.

18. As regards fiscal monopolies (heading 5122), only the amount actually transferred to the government is included in government revenues. However, if any expenditures of fiscal monopolies are considered to be government expenditures (e.g. social expenditures undertaken by fiscal monopolies at the direction of the government) they are added back for the purpose of arriving at tax revenue figures (see §61 below).

The distinction between tax and expenditure provisions[7]

19. Because this publication is concerned only with the revenue side of government operations, no account being taken of the expenditure side, a distinction has to be made between tax and expenditure provisions. Normally there is no difficulty in making this distinction as expenditures are made outside the tax system and the tax accounts and under legislation separate from the tax legislation. In borderline cases, cash flow is used to distinguish between tax provisions and expenditure provisions. Insofar as a provision affects the flow of tax payments from the taxpayer to the government, it is regarded as a tax provision and is taken into account in the data shown in this publication. A provision which does not affect this flow is seen as an expenditure provision and is disregarded in the data recorded in this publication.

20. Tax allowances, exemptions and deductions against the tax base clearly affect the amount of tax paid to the government and are therefore considered as tax provisions. At the other extreme, those subsidies which cannot be offset against tax liability and which are clearly not connected with the assessment process, do not reduce tax revenues as recorded in this publication. Tax credits are amounts deductible from tax payable (as distinct from deductions from the tax base). Two types of tax credits are distinguished, those (referred to here as wastable tax credits) which are limited to the amount of the tax liability and therefore cannot give rise to a payment by the authorities to the taxpayer, and those (referred to as non-wastable tax credits) which are not so limited, so that the excess of the credit over the tax liability can be paid to the taxpayer.[8] A wastable tax credit, like a tax allowance, clearly affects the amount of tax paid to the government, and is therefore considered as a tax provision. The practice followed for non-wastable tax credits[9] is to distinguish between the 'tax expenditure component',[10] which is that portion of the credit that is used to reduce or eliminate a taxpayer's liability, and the 'transfer component', which is the portion that exceeds the taxpayer's liability and is paid to that taxpayer. Reported tax revenues should be reduced by the amount of the tax expenditure component but not by the amount of the transfer component. In addition, the amounts of the tax expenditure and transfer components should be reported as memorandum items in the country tables. Countries that are unable to distinguish between the tax expenditure and transfer components should indicate whether or not the tax revenues have been reduced by the total of these components, and provide any available estimates of the amounts of the two components. Further information is given in Chapter 2 of the Report, which illustrates the effect of alternative treatments of non-wastable tax credits on Tax to GDP.

Calendar and fiscal years

21. National authorities whose fiscal years do not correspond to the calendar year show data, where possible, on a calendar year basis to permit maximum comparability with the data of other countries. There remain a few countries where data refer to fiscal years. For these the GDP data used in the comparative tables also correspond to the fiscal years.

A.4. General classification criteria

The main classification criteria

22. The classification of receipts among the main headings (1000, 2000, 3000, 4000, 5000 and 6000) is generally governed by the base on which the tax is levied: 1000 income, profits and capital gains; 2000 and 3000 earnings, payroll or number of employees; 4000 property; 5000 goods and services; 6000 multiple bases, other bases or unidentifiable bases. Where a tax is calculated on more than one base, the receipts are, where possible, split among the various headings (see §27 and §77). The headings 4000 and 5000 cover

not only taxes where the tax base is the property, goods or services themselves but also certain related taxes. Thus, taxes on the transfer of property are included in 4400[11] and taxes on the use of goods or on permission to perform activities in 5200. In headings 4000 and 5000 a distinction is made in certain sub-headings between recurrent and non-recurrent taxes: recurrent taxes are defined as those levied at regular intervals (usually annually) and non-recurrent taxes are levied once and for all (see also §42 to §45, §48, §49 and §75 for particular applications of this distinction).

23. Earmarking of a tax for specific purposes does not affect the classification of tax receipts. However, as explained in §34 on the classification of social security contributions, the conferment of an entitlement to social benefits is crucial to the definition of the 2000 main heading.

24. The way that a tax is levied or collected (e.g. by use of stamps) does not affect classification.

Classification of taxpayers

25. In certain sub-headings distinctions are made between different categories of taxpayers. These distinctions vary from tax to tax:

   a) *Between individuals and corporations in relation to income and net wealth taxes*

The basic distinction is that corporation income taxes, as distinct from individual income taxes, are levied on the corporation as an entity, not on the individuals who own it, and without regard to the personal circumstances of these individuals. The same distinction applies to net wealth taxes on corporations and those on individuals. Taxes paid on the profits of partnerships and the income of institutions, such as life insurance or pension funds, are classified according to the same rule. They are classified as corporate taxes (1200) if they are charged on the partnership or institution as an entity without regard to the personal circumstances of the owners. Otherwise, they are treated as individual taxes (1100). Usually, there is different legislation for the corporation taxes and for the individual taxes.[12] The distinction made here between individuals and corporations does not follow the sector classification between households, enterprises, and so on of the System of National Accounts for income and outlay accounts. The SNA classification requires certain unincorporated businesses[13] to be excluded from the household sector and included with non-financial enterprises and financial institutions. The tax on the profits of these businesses, however, cannot always be separated from the tax on the other income of their owners, or can be separated only on an arbitrary basis. No attempt at this separation is made here and the whole of the individual income tax is shown together without regard to the nature of the income chargeable.

   b) *Between households and others in relation to taxes on immovable property*

Here the distinction is that adopted by the SNA for the production and consumption expenditure accounts. The distinction is between households as consumers (i.e. excluding non-incorporated business) on the one hand and producers on the other hand. However, taxes on dwellings occupied by households, whether paid by owner-occupiers, tenants or landlords, are classified under households. This follows the common distinction made between taxes on domestic property versus taxes on business property. Some countries are not, however, in a position to make this distinction.

   c) *Between households and others in relation to motor vehicle licences*

Here the distinction is between households as consumers on the one hand and producers on the other, as in the production and consumption expenditure accounts of the SNA.

d) Between business and others in relation to the residual taxes (6000)

The distinction is the same as in c) above between producers on the one hand and households as consumers on the other hand. Taxes which are included under the heading 6000 because they involve more than one tax base or because the tax base does not fall within any of the previous categories but which are identifiable as levyable only on producers and not on households are included under 'business'. The rest of the taxes which are included under the heading 6000 are shown as 'other' or non-identified.

Surcharges

26. Receipts from surcharges in respect of particular taxes are usually classified with the receipts from the relevant tax whether or not the surcharge is temporary. If, however, the surcharge has a characteristic which would render it classifiable in a different heading of the OECD list, receipts from the surcharge are classified under that heading separately from the relevant tax.

Unidentifiable tax receipts and residual sub-headings

27. A number of cases arise where taxes cannot be identified as belonging entirely to a heading or sub-heading of the OECD classification and the following practices are applied in such cases:

a) The heading is known, but it is not known how receipts should be allocated between sub-headings: receipts are classified in the appropriate residual sub-heading (1300, 2400, 4520, 4600, 5130, 5300 or 6200).

b) It is known that the bulk of receipts from a group of taxes (usually local taxes) is derived from taxes within a particular heading or sub-heading, but some of the taxes in the group whose amount cannot be precisely ascertained may be classifiable in other headings or sub-headings: receipts are shown in the heading or sub-heading under which most of the receipts fall.

c) Neither the heading nor sub-heading of a tax (usually local) can be identified: the tax is classified in 6200 unless it is known that it is a tax on business in which case it is classified in 6100.

A.5. Commentaries on items of the list

1000 – Taxes on income, profits and capital gains

28. This heading covers taxes levied on the net income or profits (i.e. gross income minus allowable tax reliefs) of individuals and enterprises. Also covered are taxes levied on the capital gains of individuals and enterprises, and gains from gambling.

29. Included in the heading are:

a) taxes levied predominantly on income or profits, though partially on other bases. Taxes on various bases which are not predominantly income or profits are classified according to the principles laid down in §27 and §77;

b) taxes on property, which are levied on a presumed or estimated income as part of an income tax (see also §42(a), (c) and (d));

c) compulsory payments to social security fund contributions that are levied on income but do not confer an entitlement to social benefits. When such contributions do confer an entitlement to social benefits, they are included in heading 2000 (see §34);

d) receipts from integrated scheduler income tax systems are classified as a whole in this heading, even though certain of the scheduler taxes may be based upon gross income and may not take into account the personal circumstances of the taxpayer.

30. The main subdivision of this heading is between levies on individuals (1100) and those on corporate enterprises (1200). Under each subdivision a distinction is made between taxes on income and profits (1110 and 1210), and taxes on capital gains (1120 and 1220). If certain receipts cannot be identified as appropriate to either 1100 or 1200, or if in practice this distinction cannot be made (e.g. because there are no reliable data on the recipients of payments from which withholding taxes are deducted) they are classified in 1300 as not-allocable.

Treatment of credits under imputation systems

31. Under imputation systems of corporate income tax, a company's shareholders are wholly or partly relieved of their liability to income tax on dividends paid by the company out of income or profits liable to corporate income tax. In countries with such systems,[14] part of the tax on the company's profits is available to provide relief against the shareholders' own tax liability. The relief to the shareholder takes the form of a tax credit, the amount of which may be less than, equal to, or more than the shareholder's overall tax liability. If the tax credit exceeds this tax liability the excess may be payable to the shareholder. As this type of tax credit is an integral part of the imputation system of corporate income tax, any payment to the shareholders is treated as a repayment of tax and not as expenditure (compare the treatment of other tax credits described in §20).

32. As the tax credit under imputation systems (even when exceeding tax liability) is to be regarded as a tax provision, the question arises whether it should be deducted from individual income tax receipts (1110) or corporate income tax receipts (1210). In this Report, the full amount of corporate income tax paid is shown under 1210 and no imputed tax is included under 1110. Thus, the full amount of the credit reduces the amount of 1110 whether the credit results in a reduction of personal income tax liability or whether an actual refund is made because the credit exceeds the income tax liability. (Where, however, such tax credits are deducted from corporation tax in respect of dividends paid to corporations the amounts are deducted from the receipts of 1210.)

1120 and 1220 – *Taxes on capital gains*

33. These sub-headings comprise taxes imposed on capital gains, 1120 covering those levied on the gains of individuals and 1220 those levied on the gains of corporate enterprises, where receipts from such taxes can be separately identified. In many countries this is not the case and the receipts from such taxes are then classified with those from the income tax. Heading 1120 also includes taxes on gains from gambling.

2000 – *Social security contributions*

34. Classified here are all compulsory payments that confer an entitlement to receive a (contingent) future social benefit. Such payments are usually earmarked to finance social benefits and are often paid to institutions of general government that provide such benefits. However, such earmarking is not part of the definition of social security contributions and is not required for a tax to be classified here. However, conferment of an entitlement is required for a tax to be classified under this heading. So, levies on income or payroll that are earmarked for social security funds but do not confer an entitlement to benefit are excluded from this heading and shown under personal income taxes (1100) or taxes on payroll and workforce (3000). Taxes on other bases, such

as goods and services, which are earmarked for social security benefits are not shown here but are classified according to their respective bases because they generally confer no entitlement to social security benefits.

35. Contributions for the following types of social security benefits would, *inter alia*, be included: unemployment insurance benefits and supplements, accident, injury and sickness benefits, old-age, disability and survivors' pensions, family allowances, reimbursements for medical and hospital expenses or provision of hospital or medical services. Contributions may be levied on both employees and employers.

36. Contributions may be based on earnings or payroll ('on a payroll basis') or on net income after deductions and exemptions for personal circumstances ('on an income tax basis'), and the revenues from the two bases should be separately identified if possible. However, where contributions to a general social security scheme are on a payroll basis, but the contributions of particular groups (such as the self-employed) cannot be assessed on this basis and net income is used as a proxy for gross earnings, the receipts may still be classified as being on a payroll basis. In principle, this heading excludes voluntary contributions paid to social security schemes. When separately identifiable these are shown in the memorandum item on the financing of social security benefits. In practice, however, they cannot always be separately identified from compulsory contributions, in which case they are included in this heading.

37. Contributions to social insurance schemes which are not institutions of general government and to other types of insurance schemes, provident funds, pension funds, friendly societies or other saving schemes are not considered as social security contributions. Provident funds are arrangements under which the contributions of each employee and of the corresponding employer on his/her behalf are kept in a separate account earning interest and withdrawable under specific circumstances. Pension funds are separately organised schemes negotiated between employees and employers and carry provisions for different contributions and benefits, sometimes more directly tied to salary levels and length of service than under social security schemes. When contributions to these schemes are compulsory or quasi-compulsory (e.g. by virtue of agreement with professional and union organisations) they are shown in the memorandum item (refer to Chapter 4.2 of the Report).

38. Contributions by government employees and by governments in respect of their employees, to social security schemes classified within general government are included in this heading. Contributions to separate schemes for government employees, which can be regarded as replacing general social security schemes, are also regarded as taxes.[15] Where, however, a separate scheme is not seen as replacing a general scheme and has been negotiated between the government, in its role as an employer, and its employees, it is not regarded as social security and contributions to it are not regarded as taxes, even though the scheme may have been established by legislation.

39. This heading excludes 'imputed' contributions, which correspond to social benefits paid directly by employers to their employees or former employees or to their representatives (e.g. when employers are legally obliged to pay sickness benefits for a certain period).

40. Contributions are divided into those of employees (2100), employers (2200), and self-employed or non-employed (2300), and then further sub-divided according to the basis on which they are levied. Employees are defined for this purpose as all persons engaged in activities of business units, government bodies, private non-profit institutions, or other paid employment, except the proprietors and their unpaid family members in the case of unincorporated businesses. Members of the armed forces are included, irrespective of

the duration and type of their service, if they contribute to social security schemes. The contributions of employers are defined as their payments on account of their employees to social security schemes. Where employees or employers are required to continue the payment of social security contributions when the employee becomes unemployed these contributions, data permitting, are shown in 2100 and 2200 respectively. Accordingly, the sub-heading 2300 is confined to contributions paid by the self-employed and by those outside of the labour force (e.g. disabled or retired individuals).

3000 – Taxes on payroll and workforce

41.   This heading covers taxes paid by employers, employees or the self-employed either as a proportion of payroll or as a fixed amount per person, and which do not confer entitlement to social benefits. Examples of taxes classified here are the United Kingdom national insurance surcharge (introduced in 1977), the Swedish payroll tax (1969–1979), and the Austrian Contribution to the Family Burden Equalisation Fund and Community Tax.

4000 – Taxes on property

42.   This heading covers recurrent and non-recurrent taxes on the use, ownership or transfer of property. These include taxes on immovable property or net wealth, taxes on the change of ownership of property through inheritance or gift and taxes on financial and capital transactions. The following kinds of tax are excluded from this heading:

a)   taxes on capital gains resulting from the sale of a property (1120 or 1220);

b)   taxes on the use of goods or on permission to use goods or perform activities (5200); see §72;

c)   taxes on immovable property levied on the basis of a presumed net income which take into account the personal circumstances of the taxpayer. They are classified as income taxes along with taxes on income and capital gains derived from property (1100);

d)   taxes on the use of property for residence, where the tax is payable by either proprietor or tenant and the amount payable is a function of the user's personal circumstances (pay, dependants, and so on). They are classified as taxes on income (1100);

e)   taxes on building in excess of permitted maximum density, taxes on the enlargement, construction or alteration of certain buildings beyond a permitted value and taxes on building construction. They are classified as taxes on permission to perform activities (5200);

f)   taxes on the use of one's own property for special trading purposes like selling alcohol, tobacco, meat or for exploitation of land resources (e.g. United States severance taxes). They are classified as taxes on permission to perform activities (5200).

4100 – Recurrent taxes on immovable property

43.   This sub-heading covers taxes levied regularly in respect of the use or ownership of immovable property.

- these taxes are levied on land and buildings;
- they can be in the form of a percentage of an assessed property value based on a national rental income, sales price, or capitalised yield; or in terms of other characteristics of real property, (for example size or location) from which a presumed rent or capital value can be derived.

- such taxes can be levied on proprietors, tenants, or both. They can also be paid by one level of government to another level of government in respect of property under the jurisdiction of the latter.
- debts are not taken into account in the assessment of these taxes, and they differ from taxes on net wealth in this respect.

44. Taxes on immovable property are further sub-divided into those paid by households (4110) and those paid by other entities (4120), according to the criteria set out in §25(*b*) above.

4200 – Recurrent taxes on net wealth

45. This sub-heading covers taxes levied regularly (in most cases annually) on net wealth, i.e. taxes on a wide range of movable and immovable property, net of debt. It is sub-divided into taxes paid by individuals (4210) and taxes paid by corporate enterprises (4220) according to the criteria set out in §25(a) above. If separate figures exist for receipts paid by institutions, the tax payments involved are added to those paid by corporations.

4300 – Estate, inheritance and gift taxes

46. This sub-heading is divided into taxes on estates and inheritances (4310) and taxes on gifts (4320).[16] Estate taxes are charged on the amount of the total estate whereas inheritance taxes are charged on the shares of the individual recipients; in addition the latter may take into account the relationship of the individual recipients to the deceased.

4400 – Taxes on financial and capital transactions

47. This sub-heading comprises, *inter alia*, taxes on the issue, transfer, purchase and sale of securities, taxes on cheques, and taxes levied on specific legal transactions such as validation of contracts and the sale of immovable property. The heading does not include:

a) taxes on the use of goods or property or permission to perform certain activities (5200);

b) fees paid to cover court charges, charges for birth, marriage or death certificates, which are normally regarded as non-tax revenues (see §9);

c) taxes on capital gains (1000);

d) recurrent taxes on immovable property (4100);

e) recurrent taxes on net wealth (4200);

f) once-and-for-all levies on property or wealth (4500).

4500 – Other non-recurrent taxes on property[16]

48. This sub-heading covers once-and-for-all, as distinct from recurrent, levies on property. It is divided into taxes on net wealth (4510) and other non-recurrent taxes on property (4520). Heading 4510 would include taxes levied to meet emergency expenditures, or for redistribution purposes. Heading 4520 would cover taxes levied to take account of increases in land value due to permission given to develop or provision of additional local facilities by general government, any taxes on the revaluation of capital and once-and-for-all taxes on particular items of property.

4600 – Other recurrent taxes on property

49. These rarely exist in OECD member countries, but the heading would include taxes on goods such as cattle, jewellery, windows, and other external signs of wealth.

5000 – *Taxes on goods and services*

50. All taxes and duties levied on the production, extraction, sale, transfer, leasing or delivery of goods, and the rendering of services (5100), or in respect of the use of goods or permission to use goods or to perform activities (5200) are included here. The heading thus covers:

a) multi-stage cumulative taxes;

b) general sales taxes – whether levied at manufacture/production, wholesale or retail level;

c) value-added taxes;

d) excises;

e) taxes levied on the import and export of goods;

f) taxes levied in respect of the use of goods and taxes on permission to use goods, or perform certain activities;

g) taxes on the extraction, processing or production of minerals and other products.

51. Borderline cases between this heading and heading 4000 (taxes on property) and 6100 (other taxes on business) are referred to in §42, §47 and §74. Residual sub-headings (5300) and (5130) cover tax receipts which cannot be allocated between 5100 and 5200 and between 5110 and 5120, respectively; see §27.

5100 – *Taxes on the production, sale, transfer, leasing and delivery of goods and rendering of services*

52. This sub-heading consists of all taxes, levied on transactions in goods and services on the basis of their intrinsic characteristics (e.g. value, weight of tobacco, strength of alcohol, and so on) as distinct from taxes imposed on the use of goods, or permission to use goods or perform activities, which fall under 5200.

5110 – *General taxes on goods and services*

53. This sub-heading includes all taxes, other than import and export duties (5123 and 5124), levied on the production, leasing, transfer, delivery or sales of a wide range of goods and/or the rendering of a wide range of services, irrespective of whether they are domestically produced or imported and irrespective of the stage of production or distribution at which they are levied. It thus covers value-added taxes, sales taxes and multi-stage cumulative taxes. Receipts from border adjustments in respect of such taxes when goods are imported are added to gross receipts for this category, and repayments of such taxes when goods are exported are deducted. These taxes are subdivided into 5111 value-added taxes, 5112 sales taxes, 5113 other general taxes on goods and services.

54. Borderline cases arise between this heading and taxes on specific goods (5120) when taxes are levied on a large number of goods, for example, the United Kingdom purchase tax (repealed in 1973) and the Japanese commodity tax (repealed in 1988). In conformity with national views, the former United Kingdom purchase tax is classified as a general tax (5112) and the former Japanese commodity tax as excises (5121).

5111 – *Value-added taxes*

55. All general consumption taxes charged on value-added are classified in this sub-heading, irrespective of the method of deduction and the stages at which the taxes are levied. In practice, all OECD countries with value-added taxes normally allow immediate deduction of taxes on purchases by all but the final consumer and impose

tax at all stages. In some countries the heading may include certain taxes, such as those on financial and insurance activities, either because receipts from them cannot be identified separately from those from the value-added tax, or because they are regarded as an integral part of the value-added tax, even though similar taxes in other countries might be classified elsewhere (e.g. 5126 as taxes on services or 4400 as taxes on financial and capital transactions).

5112 – Sales taxes

56. All general taxes levied at one stage only, whether at manufacturing or production, wholesale or retail stage are classified here.

5113 – Other general taxes on goods and services

57. This sub-heading covers multi-stage cumulative taxes (also know as 'cascade taxes') where tax is levied each time a transaction takes place without deduction for tax paid on inputs, and also those general consumption taxes where elements of value-added, sales or cascade taxes are combined.

5120 – Taxes on specific goods and services

58. Excises, profits generated and transferred from fiscal monopolies, and customs and imports duties as well as taxes on exports, foreign exchange transactions, investment goods and betting stakes and special taxes on services, which do not form part of a general tax of 5110, are included in this category.

5121 – Excises

59. Excises are taxes levied on particular products, or on a limited range of products, which are not classifiable under 5110 (general taxes), 5123 (import duties) and 5124 (export duties). They may be imposed at any stage of production or distribution and are usually assessed by reference to the weight or strength or quantity of the product, but sometimes by reference to value. Thus, special taxes on, for example, sugar, beetroot, matches, chocolates, and taxes at varying rates on a certain range of goods, as well as those levied in most countries on tobacco goods, alcoholic drinks and hydrocarbon oils and other energy sources, are included in this sub-heading.

60. Excises are distinguished from:

a) 5110 (general taxes). This is discussed in §53-54;

b) 5123 (import duties). If a tax collected principally on imported goods also applies, or would apply, under the law by which the tax is imposed to comparable home-produced goods, the receipts there from would be classified as excises (5121). This principle applies even if there is no comparable home production or no possibility of it (see also §64);

c) 5126 (taxes on services). The problem here arises in respect of taxes on electricity, gas and energy. All of these are regarded as taxes on goods and are included under 5121.

5122 – Profits of fiscal monopolies

61. This sub-heading covers that part of the profits of fiscal monopolies which is transferred to general government or which is used to finance any expenditures considered to be government expenditures (see §18). Amounts are shown when they are transferred to general government or used to make expenditures considered to be government expenditures

62. Fiscal monopolies reflect the exercise of the taxing power of government by the use of monopoly powers. Fiscal monopolies are non-financial public enterprises exercising a monopoly in most cases over the production or distribution of tobacco, alcoholic beverages, salt, matches, playing cards and petroleum or agricultural products (i.e. on the kind of products which are likely to be, alternatively or additionally, subject to the excises of 5121), to raise the government revenues which in other countries are gathered through taxes on dealings in such commodities by private business units. The government monopoly may be at the production stage or, as in the case of government-owned and controlled liquor stores, at the distribution stage.

63. Fiscal monopolies are distinguished from public utilities such as rail transport, electricity, post offices, and other communications, which may enjoy a monopoly or quasi-monopoly position but where the primary purpose is normally to provide basic services rather than to raise revenue for government. Transfers from such other public enterprises to the government are considered as non-tax revenues. The traditional concept of fiscal monopoly is not generally extended to include state lotteries, the profits of which are usually accordingly regarded as non-tax revenues. However, they can be included as tax revenues if the prime reason for their operation is to raise revenues to finance government expenditure. Fiscal monopoly profits are distinguished from export and import monopoly profits (5127) transferred from marketing boards or other enterprises dealing with international trade.

5123 – *Customs and other import duties*

64. Taxes, stamp duties and surcharges restricted by law to imported products are included here. Also included are levies on imported agricultural products which are imposed in member countries of the European Union and amounts paid by certain of these countries under the Monetary Compensation Accounts (MCA) system.[17] Starting from 1998, customs duties collected by European Union member states on behalf of the European Union are no longer reported under this heading in the country tables (in Chapter 4 of the Report). Excluded here are taxes collected on imports as part of a general tax on goods and services, or an excise applicable to both imported and domestically produced goods.

5124 – *Taxes on exports*

65. In the 1970s, export duties were levied in Australia, Canada and Portugal as a regular measure and they have been used in Finland for counter-cyclical purposes. Some member countries of the European Union pay, as part of the MCA system, a levy on exports (see note 16 to §64). Where these amounts are identifiable, they are shown in this heading. This heading does not include repayments of general consumption taxes or excises or customs duties on exported goods, which should be deducted from the gross receipts under 5110, 5121 or 5123, as appropriate.

5125 – *Taxes on investment goods*

66. This sub-heading covers taxes on investment goods, such as machinery. These taxes may be imposed for a number of years or temporarily for counter-cyclical purposes. Taxes on industrial inputs which are also levied on consumers [e.g. the Swedish energy tax which is classified under (5121)] are not included here.

5126 – *Taxes on specific services*

67. All taxes assessed on the payment for specific services, such as taxes on insurance premiums, banking services, gambling and betting stakes (e.g. from horse races, football pools, lottery tickets), transport, entertainment, restaurant and advertising charges, fall into this category. Taxes levied on the gross income of companies providing the service

(e.g. gross insurance premiums or gambling stakes received by the company) are also classified under this heading. Tax revenues from bank levies and payments to deposit insurance and financial stability schemes are provisionally included here for the 2012 edition. The detailed classification is set out in paragraph 104.

68. Excluded from this sub-heading are:

   a) taxes on services forming part of a general tax on goods and services (5110);

   b) taxes on electricity, gas and energy (5121 as excises);

   c) taxes on individual gains from gambling (1120 as taxes on capital gains of individuals and non-corporate enterprises) and lump-sum taxes on the transfer of private lotteries or on the permission to set up lotteries (5200);[18]

   d) taxes on cheques and on the issue, transfer or redemption of securities (4400 as taxes on financial and capital transactions).

5127 – Other taxes on international trade and transactions

69. This sub-heading covers revenue received by the government from the purchase and sale of foreign exchange at different rates. When the government exercises monopoly powers to extract a margin between the purchase and sales price of foreign exchange, other than to cover administrative costs, the revenue derived constitutes a compulsory levy exacted in indeterminate proportions from both purchaser and seller of foreign exchange. It is the common equivalent of an import duty and export duty levied in a single exchange rate system or of a tax on the sale or purchase of foreign exchange. Like the profits of fiscal monopolies and import or export monopolies transferred to government, it represents the exercise of monopoly powers for tax purposes and is included in tax revenues.

70. The sub-heading covers also the profits of export or import monopolies, which do not however exist in OECD countries, taxes on purchase or sale of foreign exchange, and any other taxes levied specifically on international trade or transactions.

5128 – Other taxes on specific goods and services

71. This item includes taxes on the extraction of minerals, fossil fuels and other exhaustible resources from deposits owned privately or by another government together with any other unidentifiable receipts from taxes on specific goods and services. Taxes on the extraction of exhaustible resources are usually a fixed amount per unit of quality or weight, but can be a percentage of value. The taxes are recorded when the resources are extracted. Payments from the extraction of exhaustible resources from deposits owned by the government unit receiving the payment are classified as rent.

5200 – Taxes on use of goods or on permission to use goods or perform activities

72. This sub-heading covers taxes which are levied in respect of the use of goods as distinct from taxes on the goods themselves. Unlike the latter taxes – reported under 5100 –, they are not assessed on the value of the goods but usually as fixed amounts. Taxes on permission to use goods or to perform activities are also included here, as are pollution taxes not based upon the value of particular goods. It is sometimes difficult to distinguish between compulsory user charges and licence fees which are regarded as taxes and those which are excluded as non-tax revenues. The criteria which are employed are noted in §9–10.

73. Although the sub-heading refers to the 'use' of goods, registration of ownership rather than use may be what generates liability to tax, so that the taxes of this heading may apply to the ownership of animals or goods rather than their use (e.g. race horses, dogs and motor vehicles) and may apply even to unusable goods (e.g. unusable motor vehicles or guns).

74. Borderline cases arise with:

a) taxes on the permission to perform business activities which are levied on a combined income, payroll or turnover base and, accordingly, are classified following the rules in §77;

b) taxes on the ownership or use of property of headings 4100, 4200 and 4600. The heading 4100 is confined to taxes on the ownership or tenancy of immovable property and – unlike the taxes of 5200 – they are related to the value of the property. The net wealth taxes and taxes on chattels of 4200 and 4600 respectively are confined to the ownership rather than the use of assets, apply to groups of assets rather than particular goods and again are related to the value of the assets.

5210 – Recurrent taxes on use of goods and on permission to use goods or perform activities

75. The principal characteristic of taxes classified here is that they are levied at regular intervals and that they are usually fixed amounts. The most important item in terms of revenue receipts is vehicle licence taxes. This sub-heading also covers taxes on permission to hunt, shoot, fish or to sell certain products and taxes on the ownership of dogs and on the performance of certain services, provided that they meet the criteria set out in §9–10. The sub-divisions of 5210 are user taxes on motor vehicles paid by households (5211) and those paid by others (5212).[19] Sub-heading 5213 covers dog licences and user charges for permission to perform activities such as selling meat or liquor when the levies are on a recurring basis. It also covers recurrent general licences for hunting, shooting and fishing where the right to carry out these activities is not granted as part of a normal commercial transaction (e.g. the granting of the licence is not accompanied by the right to use a specific area which is owned by government).

5220 – Non-recurrent taxes on use of goods and on permission to use goods or perform activities

76. This section covers non-recurrent taxes levied on the use of goods or on permission to use goods or perform activities and taxes levied each time goods are used. It includes taxes levied on the emission or discharge into the environment of noxious gases, liquids or other harmful substances.

- Payments for tradable emission permits issued by governments under cap and trade schemes should be recorded here at the time the emissions occur. No revenue should be recorded for permits that governments issue free of charge. The accrual basis of recording means that there can be a timing difference between the cash being received by government for the permits and the time the emission occurs. In the national accounts, this timing gives rise to a financial liability for government during the period.

- Payments made for the collection and disposal of waste or noxious substances by public authorities should be excluded as they constitute a sale of services to enterprises.

77. Other taxes falling under heading 5200 that are not levied recurrently are also included here. Thus, once-and-for-all payments for permission to sell liquor or tobacco or to set up betting shops are included provided they meet the criteria set out in §9–10.

6000 – Other taxes

78. Taxes levied on a base, or bases, other than those described under headings 1000, 3000, 4000 and 5000, or on bases of which none could be regarded as being predominantly the same as that of any one of these headings, are covered here. As regards taxes levied on a multiple base, if it is possible to estimate receipts related to each base (e.g. the Austrian and German 'Gewerbesteuer') this is done and the separate amounts included under the appropriate headings. If the separate amounts cannot be estimated, but it is

known that most of the receipts are derived from one base, the whole of the receipts are classified according to that base. If neither of these procedures can be followed, they are classified here. The sub-headings may also include receipts from taxes which governments are unable to identify or isolate (see §27). Included here also are fines and penalties paid for infringement of regulations relating to taxes but not identifiable as relating to a particular category of taxes (see §14). A subdivision is made between taxes levied wholly or predominantly on business (6100) and those levied on others (6200).

A.6. Conciliation with National Accounts

79. This section of the tables provides a re-conciliation between the OECD calculation of total tax revenues and the total of all taxes and social contributions paid to general government as recorded in the country's National Accounts. Where the country is a member of the European Union (EU), the comparison is between the OECD calculation of total tax revenues and the sum of tax revenues and social contributions recorded in the combination of the general government and the institutions of the EU sectors of the National Accounts.

A.7. Memorandum item on the financing of social security benefits

80. In view of the varying relationship between taxation and social security contributions and the cases referred to in §34 to §40, a memorandum item collects together all payments earmarked for social security-type benefits, other than voluntary payments to the private sector. Data are presented as follows (refer Chapter 4.2 of the Report):

a) Taxes of 2000 series.

b) Taxes earmarked for social security benefits.

c) Voluntary contributions to the government.

d) Compulsory contributions to the private sector.

Guidance on the breakdown of (a) to (d) above is provided in §34 to §40.

A.8. Memorandum item on identifiable taxes paid by government

81. Identifiable taxes actually paid by government are presented in a memorandum item classified by the main headings of the OECD classification of taxes. In the vast majority of countries, only social security contributions and payroll taxes paid by government can be identified. These are, however, usually the most important taxes paid by governments (refer to Chapter 4.3 of the Report).

A.9. Relation of OECD classification of taxes to national accounting systems

82. A system of national accounts (SNA) seeks to provide a coherent framework for recording and presenting the main flows relating respectively to production, consumption, accumulation and external transactions of a given economic area, usually a country or a major region within a country. Government revenues are an important part of the transactions recorded in SNA. The final version of the 2008 SNA was jointly published by five international organisations: the United Nations, the International Monetary Fund, the European Union, the Organisation for Economic Co-operation and Development, and the World Bank in August 2009. The *System* is a comprehensive, consistent and flexible set of macroeconomic accounts. It is designed for use in countries with market economies, whatever their stage of economic development, and also in countries in transition to market economies. The important parts of the SNA's conceptual framework and its definitions of the various sectors of the economy have been reflected in the OECD's classification of taxes.

83. There are, however, some differences between the OECD classification of taxes and SNA concepts that are listed below. They arise because the aim of the former is to provide the maximum disaggregation of statistical data on what are generally regarded as taxes by tax administrations.

    a) OECD includes compulsory social security contributions paid to general government in total tax revenues. Imputed and voluntary contributions plus those paid to private funds are not treated as taxes (§7 and §8 above);

    b) there are different points of view on whether or not some levies and fees are classified as taxes (§9 and §10 above);

    c) OECD excludes imputed taxes or subsidies resulting from the operation of official multiple exchange rates or from the central bank paying a rate of interest on required reserves that is different from other market rates;

    d) there are differences in the treatment of non-wastable tax credits

84. As noted in §1 and §2, headings 1000 to 6000 of the OECD list of taxes cover all unrequited payments to general government, other than compulsory loans and fines. Such unrequited payments including fines, but excluding compulsory loans can be obtained from adding together the following figures in the 2008 SNA

- value-added type taxes (D.211);
- taxes and duties on imports, excluding VAT (D.212);
- export taxes (D.213);
- taxes on products, excluding VAT, import and export taxes (D.214);
- other taxes on production (D.29);
- taxes on income (D.51);
- other current taxes (D.59);
- social contributions (D.61), excluding voluntary contributions;
- capital taxes (D.91).

A.10. The OECD classification of taxes and the International Monetary Fund (GFS) system

85. The coverage and valuation of tax revenues in the GFS system and the 2008 SNA are very similar. Therefore, the differences between the OECD classification and that of the 2008 SNA (see §83 above) also apply to the GFS. In addition the International Monetary Fund subdivides the OECD 5000 heading into section IV (Domestic Taxes on Goods and Services) and section V (Taxes on International Trade and Transactions). This reflects the fact that while the latter usually yield insignificant amounts of revenue in OECD countries, this is not the case in many non-OECD countries.

A.11. Comparison of the OECD classification of taxes with other international classifications

86. The table below describes an item by item comparison of the OECD classification of taxes and the classifications used in the following:

    i) System of National Accounts (2008 SNA);

    ii) European System of Accounts (1995 ESA);

    iii) IMF *Government Finance Statistics Manual* (GFSM2001).

87. These comparisons represent those that would be expected to apply in the majority of cases. However in practice some flexibility should be used in their application. This is because in particular cases, countries can adopt varying approaches to the classification of revenues in National Accounts.

OECD Classification				2008 SNA	2010 ESA	GFSM2014
1000	Taxes on income, profits and capital gains					
	1100 Individuals					
		1110 Income/profits		D51-8.61a	D51A	1111
		1120 Capital gains		D51-8.61c,d	D51C,D	1111
	1200 Corporations					
		1210 Income/profits		D51-8.61b	D51B	1112
		1220 Capital gains		D51-8.61c	D51C	1112
	1300 Unallocable as between 1100 and 1200					1113
2000	Social security contributions					
	2100 Employees			D613-8.85	D613	1211
	2200 Employers			D611-8.83	D611	1212
	2300 Self-employed, non-employed			D613-8.85	D613	1213
	2400 Unallocable as between 2100, 2200 and 2300					1214
3000	Taxes on payroll and workforce			D29-7.97a	D29C	112
4000	Taxes on property					
	4100 Recurrent taxes on immovable property					
		4110 Households		D59-8.63a	D59A	1131
		4120 Other		D29-7.97b	D29A	1131
	4200 Recurrent net wealth taxes					
		4210 Individual		D59-8.63b	D59A	1132
		4220 Corporations		D59-8.63b	D59A	1132
	4300 Estate, inheritance and gift taxes					
		4310 Estate and inheritance taxes		D91-10.207b	D91A	1133
		4320 Gift taxes		D91-10.207b	D91A	1133
	4400 Taxes on financial and capital transactions			D59-7.96d; D29-7.97e	D214B,C	114114; 1161
	4500 Other non-recurrent taxes on property			D91-10.207a	D91B	1135
	4600 Other recurrent taxes on property			D59-8.63c	D59A	1136
5000	Taxes on goods and services					
	5100 Taxes on production, sale and transfer of goods and services					
		5110 General taxes on goods and services				
			5111 Value-added taxes	D211-7.89	D211; D29G	11411
			5112 Sales taxes	D2122-7.94a; D214-7.96a	D21224; D214I	11412
			5113 Other general taxes on goods and services	D214-7.96a	D214I	11413
		5120 Taxes on specific goods and services				
			5121 Excises	D2122-7.94b; D214-7.96b	D21223; D214A,B,D	1142
			5122 Profits of fiscal monopolies	D214-7.96e	D214J	1143
			5123 Customs/import duties	D2121-7.93	D2121; D21221,2	1151
			5124 On exports	D213-7.95a	D214K	1152-4
			5125 On investment goods			
			5126 On specific services	D2122-7.94c; D214-7.96c	D21225; D214E,F,G; D29F	1144; 1156
			5127 Other taxes on international trade and transactions	D2122-7.94d D29-7.95b D29-7.97g D59-8.64d	D21226; D29D; D59E	1153 1155-6
			5128 Other taxes on specific goods and services			1146
		5130 Unallocable as between 5110 and 5120				
	5200 Taxes on use of goods and on permission to use goods or perform activities					
		5210 Recurrent taxes on use of goods and on permission to use goods or perform activities				
			5211 Motor vehicle taxes households	D59-8.64c	D59D	11451
			5212 Motor vehicles taxes others	D29-7.97d	D214D; D29B	11451
			5213 Other recurrent taxes on use of goods and on permission to use goods or perform activities	D29-7.97c,d,f D59-8.64c	D29B,E,F; D59D	11452
		5220 Non-recurrent taxes on permission to use goods or perform activities				
	5300 Unallocable as between 5100 and 5200					
6000	Other taxes					
	6100 Payable solely by business					1161
	6200 Payable by other than business, or unidentifiable			D59-8.64a,b	D59B,C	1162

A.12. Attribution of tax revenues by sub-sectors of general government

88. The OECD classification requires a breakdown of tax revenues by sub-sectors of government. The definition of each sub-sector and the criteria to be used to attribute tax revenues between these sub-sectors are set out below. They follow the guidance of the 2008 SNA and GFSM 2014.

Sub-sectors of general government to be identified

a) Central government

89. The central government sub-sector includes all governmental departments, offices, establishments and other bodies which are agencies or instruments of the central authority whose competence extends over the whole territory, with the exception of the administration of social security funds.Central government therefore has the authority to impose taxes on all resident and non-resident units engaged in economic activities within the country.

b) State, provincial or regional government

90. This sub-sector consists of intermediate units of government exercising a competence at a level below that of central government. It includes all such units operating independently of central government in a part of a country's territory encompassing a number of smaller localities, with the exception of the administration of social security funds. In unitary countries, regional governments may be considered to have a separate existence where they have substantial autonomy to raise a significant proportion of their revenues from sources within their control and their officers are independent of external administrative control in the actual operation of the unit's activities.

91. At present, federal countries comprise the majority of cases where revenues attributed to intermediate units of government are identified separately. Spain is the only unitary country in this position. In the remaining unitary countries, regional revenues are included with those of local governments.

c) Local government

92. This sub-sector includes all other units of government exercising an independent competence in part of the territory of a country, with the exception of the administration of social security funds. It encompasses various urban and/or rural jurisdictions (e.g. local authorities, municipalities, cities, boroughs, districts).

d) Social security funds

93. Social security funds form a separate sub-sector of general government. The social security sub-sector is defined in the 2008 SNA by the following extracts from paragraphs 4.124 to 4.126 and 4.147:

"Social security schemes are social insurance schemes covering the community as a whole or large section of the community that are imposed and controlled by government units. The schemes cover a wide variety of programmes, providing benefits in cash or in kind for old age, invalidity or death, survivors, sickness and maternity, work injury, unemployment, family allowance, health care, etc. There is not necessarily a direct link between the amount of the contribution paid by an individual and the benefits he or she may receive." (Paragraph 4.124).

"When social security schemes are separately organised from the other activities of government units and hold their assets and liabilities separately from the latter and engage in financial transactions on their own account they qualify as institutional units that are described as social security funds." (Paragraph 4.125).

"The amounts raised, and paid out, in social security contributions and benefits may be deliberately varied in order to achieve objectives of government policy that have no direct connection with the concept of social security as a scheme to provide social benefits to members of the community. They may be raised or lowered in order to influence the level of aggregate demand in the economy, for example. Nevertheless, so long as they remain separately constituted funds, they must be treated as separate institutional units in the SNA." (Paragraph 4.126).

"The social security funds sub-sector (of general government) consists of the social security funds operating at all levels of government. Such funds are social insurance schemes covering the community as a whole or large section of the community that are imposed by government units." (Paragraph 4.147).

94. This definition of social security funds is followed in the OECD classification with the two following exceptions which are excluded:

- Schemes imposed by government and operated by bodies outside the general government sector, as defined in §3 of this manual; and
- Schemes to which all contributions are voluntary.

Supra-national authorities

95. This sub-sector covers the revenue-raising operations of supra-national authorities within a country. In practice, the only relevant supra-national authority in the OECD area is that of the institutions of the European Union (EU). As from 1998, supra-national authorities are no longer included in the *Revenue Statistics*, to achieve consistency with the SNA definition of general government which excludes them. For example, income taxes and social security contributions collected by European Institutions and paid by European civil servants who are resident of EU member countries should not be included. However the specific levies paid by the member states of the EU continue to be included in total tax revenues and they are shown under this heading.

Criteria to be used for the attribution of tax revenues

96. When a government collects taxes and pays them over in whole or in part to other governments, it is necessary to determine whether the revenues should be considered to be those of the collecting government which it distributes to others as grants, or those of the beneficiary governments which the collecting government receives and passes on only as their agent. The criteria to be used in the attribution of revenues are set out in §97 to §100 which replicate paragraphs 3.70 to 3.73 from the 2008 SNA

97. In general, a tax is attributed to the government unit that:

a) exercises the authority to impose the tax (either as a principal or through the delegated authority of the principal);

b) has final discretion to set and vary the rate of the tax.

98. Where an amount is collected by one government for and on behalf of another government, and the latter government has the authority to impose the tax, and set and vary its rate, then the former is acting as an agent for the latter and the tax is reassigned. Any amount retained by the collecting government as a collection charge should be treated as a payment for a service. Any other amount retained by the collecting government, such as under a tax-sharing arrangement, should be treated as a current

grant. If the collecting government was delegated the authority to set and vary the rate, then the amount collected should be treated as tax revenue of this government.

99. Where different governments jointly and equally set the rate of a tax and jointly and equally decide on the distribution of the proceeds, with no individual government having ultimate overriding authority, then the tax revenues are attributed to each government according to its respective share of the proceeds. If an arrangement allows one government unit to exercise ultimate overriding authority, then all of the tax revenue is attributed to that unit.

100. There may also be the circumstance where a tax is imposed under the constitutional or other authority of one government, but other governments individually set the tax rate in their jurisdictions. The proceeds of the tax generated in each respective government's jurisdiction are attributed as tax revenues of that government.

Levies paid by member states of the European Union

101. The levies paid by the member states of the EU take the form of special levies which include:

a) custom duties and levies on agricultural goods (5123);

b) gross monetary compensation accounts (5123 if relating to imports and 5124 if relating to exports); and

c) Steel, coal, sugar and milk levies (5128).

102. The custom duties collected by member states on behalf of the EU are recorded:

- on a gross of collection fee basis;
- using figures adjusted so that duties are shown on a 'final destination' as opposed to a 'country of first entry' basis where such adjustments can be made. These adjustments concern in particular duties collected at important (sea) ports. Although the EU duties are collected by the authorities of the country of first entry, when possible these duties should be excluded from the revenue of the collecting country and be included in the revenue of the country of final destination.

103. This is the specific EU levy that most clearly conforms to the attribution criterion described in §95 above. Consequently as from 1998, these amounts are footnoted as a memorandum item to the EU member state country tables (in Chapter 4) and no longer shown under heading 5123. However the figures are included in the total tax revenue figures on the top line for all the relevant years shown in the tables.

A.13. Provisional classification of revenues from bank levies and payments to deposit insurance and financial stability schemes

104. The OECD have adopted the following interim approach to reporting revenue from bank levies plus deposit insurance and stability fees for the 2012 and subsequent editions of *OECD Revenue Statistics*. It is recommended that the amounts should be recorded under category 5126.

- Compulsory payments of stability fees, bank levies and deposit insurance should generally be treated as tax revenues where the payments are made to General Government and allocated to the governments' consolidated or general funds so that the Government is free to make immediate use of the money for the purposes that it chooses. This principle would apply regardless of whether the Government is promising to make payments to guarantee the banks' customer deposits in some future contingency.

- If the compulsory payments are made to general government and placed in funds that are earmarked to be entirely channelled back to the sector of the economy that comprises the companies that are subject to the payment, they would still generally be treated as tax revenues on the grounds that the funds would be available for the government and would reduce its budget deficit, the fee is unrequited for an individual entity and the amounts raised could be unrelated to any eventual pay out to depositors or expenditure on wider support for the financial sector.

- Payments to made to the smaller long-standing schemes for insuring 'retail' deposits, where the payment levels are consistent with the costs of insurance should be classified as fee for service.

- Any payments which involve governments realising the assets of a failed institution or receiving a priority claim on its assets in liquidation in order to fund payments of compensation to customers for their lost deposits would be treated as a fee for a service as opposed to tax revenues.

- Compulsory payments that are made to funds operated outside the government sector and non-state institutions backed by the deposit takers and all payments to voluntary schemes should not be treated as tax revenues.

Notes

1. References in this OECD Interpretative Guide to Sections or Parts of "this Report" refer to OECD (2016a), *Revenue Statistics 2016*, OECD Publishing, Paris.

2. All references to SNA are to the 2008 edition.

3. See section A.12 of this guide for a discussion of the concept of agency capacity.

4. It is usually possible to identify amounts of social security contributions and payroll taxes, but not other taxes paid by government.

5. If, however, a levy which is considered as non-tax revenue by most countries is regarded as a tax – or raises substantial revenue – in one or more countries, the amounts collected are footnoted at the end of the relevant country tables, even though the amounts are not included in total tax revenues.

6. Names, however, can frequently be misleading. For example, though a passport fee would normally be considered a non-tax revenue, if a supplementary levy on passports (as is the case in Portugal) were imposed in order to raise substantial amounts of revenue relative to the cost of providing the passport, the levy would be regarded as a tax under 5200.

7. A more detailed explanation of this distinction can be found in the special feature, "Current issues in reporting tax revenues", in the 2001 edition of the *Revenue Statistics*.

8. Sometimes the terms "non-refundable" and "refundable" are used, but it may be considered illogical to talk of "refundable" when nothing has been paid.

9. A different treatment, however, is accorded to non-wastable tax credits under imputation systems of corporate income tax (§31–33).

10. This is not strictly a true tax expenditure in the formal sense. Such tax expenditures require identification of a benchmark tax system for each country or, preferably, a common international benchmark. In practice it has not been possible to reach agreement on a common international benchmark.

11. Unless based on the profit made on a sale, in which case they would be classified as capital gains taxes under 1120 or 1220.

12. In some countries the same legislation applies to both individual and corporate enterprises for particular taxes on income. However, the receipts from such taxes are usually allocable between individuals and enterprises and can therefore be shown in the appropriate sub-heading.

13. For example, "...sufficiently self-contained and independent that they behave in the same way as corporations.......(including) keeping a complete set of accounts" (2008 SNA, section 4.44).

14. In Canada – a country also referred to as having an imputation system – the (wastable) tax credit for the shareholder is in respect of domestic corporation tax deemed to have been paid whether or not a corporation tax liability has arisen. As there is no integral connection between the corporation tax liability and the credit given against income tax under such systems, these credits for dividends are treated, along with other tax credits, on the lines described in §20.

15. This may also apply where a scheme for government employees existed prior to the introduction of a general social security scheme.

16. In the 2008 SNA these are regarded as capital transfers and not as taxes (see section A.8).

17. This is the system by which the European Union adjusts for differences between the exchange rates used to determine prices under the Common Market Agricultural Policy and actual exchange rates. Payments under the system may relate to imports or exports and where these amounts are separately identifiable they are shown under the appropriate heading (5123 or 5124). In this Report, these amounts are shown gross (i.e. without deducting any subsidies paid out under the MCA system).

18. Transfers of profits of State lotteries are regarded as non-tax revenues (see also §63).

19. See §25(c) as regards this distinction.

ORGANISATION FOR ECONOMIC CO-OPERATION AND DEVELOPMENT

The OECD is a unique forum where governments work together to address the economic, social and environmental challenges of globalisation. The OECD is also at the forefront of efforts to understand and to help governments respond to new developments and concerns, such as corporate governance, the information economy and the challenges of an ageing population. The Organisation provides a setting where governments can compare policy experiences, seek answers to common problems, identify good practice and work to co-ordinate domestic and international policies.

The OECD member countries are: Australia, Austria, Belgium, Canada, Chile, the Czech Republic, Denmark, Estonia, Finland, France, Germany, Greece, Hungary, Iceland, Ireland, Israel, Italy, Japan, Korea, Latvia, Luxembourg, Mexico, the Netherlands, New Zealand, Norway, Poland, Portugal, the Slovak Republic, Slovenia, Spain, Sweden, Switzerland, Turkey, the United Kingdom and the United States. The European Union takes part in the work of the OECD.

OECD Publishing disseminates widely the results of the Organisation's statistics gathering and research on economic, social and environmental issues, as well as the conventions, guidelines and standards agreed by its members.

CENTRE FOR TAX POLICY AND ADMINISTRATION

The Centre for Tax Policy and Administration (CTPA) is the focal point for the OECD's work on taxation. The Centre provides technical expertise and support to the Committee on Fiscal Affairs and examines all aspects of taxation other than macro-fiscal policy. Its work covers international and domestic tax issues, direct and indirect taxes, tax policy and tax administration. CTPA also carries out an extensive global programme of dialogue between OECD and non-OECD tax officials through events held annually on the full range of OECD work, bringing together over 100 non-OECD economies. For information on the Centre for Tax Policy and Administration, please visit *www.oecd.org/tax*.

OECD DEVELOPMENT CENTRE

The OECD Development Centre was established in 1962 as an independent platform for knowledge sharing and policy dialogue between OECD member countries and developing economies, allowing these countries to interact on an equal footing. Today, 27 OECD countries and 25 non-OECD countries are members of the Centre. The Centre draws attention to emerging systemic issues likely to have an impact on global development and more specific development challenges faced by today's developing and emerging economies. It uses evidence-based analysis and strategic partnerships to help countries formulate innovative policy solutions to the global challenges of development.

For more information on the Centre, please see *www.oecd.org/dev*.

OECD PUBLISHING, 2, rue André-Pascal, 75775 PARIS CEDEX16
(23 2017 081 P1) ISBN 978-92-64-27893-6 – 2017